GOOD FAT COOKING

GOOD FAT COOKING

Recipes for a Flavor-Packed, Healthy Life

Franklin Becker and Peter Kaminsky

RODALE

Rodale books may be purchased for business or promotional use or for special sales. For information, please write to:
Special Markets Department, Rodale Inc., 733 Third Avenue, New York, NY 10017

Printed in the United States of America

Rodale Inc. makes every effort to use acid-free ∞, recycled paper ♻.

Photographs by Mark Jordan

Illustrations by Lindsey Spinks

Book design by Christina Gaugler

Library of Congress Cataloging-in-Publication Data is on file with the publisher.

ISBN 978-1-60961-552-9

Distributed to the trade by Macmillan

2 4 6 8 10 9 7 5 3 1 hardcover

We inspire and enable people to improve their lives and the world around them.
rodalebooks.com

For my boys, Sean and Rory:
You are my driving force.
I love you both with all my heart and soul.
Thank you for putting up with Daddy
and making me proud.

CONTENTS

Foreword by Jonathan Waxman · ix

Introduction: Friendly Fat · xv

Chef's Pantry: My Go-To Ingredients · xxvii

CHAPTER 1: SALADS • 1

CHAPTER 2: SOUPS • 23

CHAPTER 3: MOSTLY GRAINS,
MOSTLY GLUTEN-FREE • 33

CHAPTER 4: SEAFOOD • 51

CHAPTER 5:
POULTRY AND MEAT • 95

CHAPTER 6:
COOKED VEGETABLES • 117

CHAPTER 7: DESSERTS • 151

CHAPTER 8:
NIBBLES AND NOSHES • 163

Common Measurements and Equivalents · 174

Acknowledgments · 176

Index · 177

Notes · 186

FOREWORD

After I closed my Manhattan restaurant, Jams, in the late 1980s, I went out to California and opened Table 29 in Napa Valley; by the time I returned to the city in the early 1990s, I didn't really know any of New York's new young chefs. But one name kept popping up all the time: Franklin Becker. I heard his name a lot; he had worked for Bobby Flay, and people spoke very highly of him. About 7 or 8 years later, Franklin reached out to me to do one of his Autism Speaks events, and we became fast friends after that.

Like Franklin, I'm into simple cooking and simple food.

Like Franklin, in terms of cooking styles, I'm into simple cooking and simple food. I always laugh at recipes—especially in cookbooks—that are so complicated, and mired in many steps; in a way I guess those kinds of cookbooks are good for people who can't sleep at night. I like food that is seasonal, simple, rustic, and combined with a bit of artfulness . . . but not too much. And I also like to cook things that I can produce pretty easily; I just don't like to fuss around too much. On the one hand, I don't really have the time, and on the other, I don't think that food gets better when you fuss with it. And I think that Franklin really shares that spirit.

> I like food that is seasonal, simple, rustic, and combined with a bit of artfulness . . . but not too much. I don't think that food gets better when you fuss with it. And I think that Franklin really shares that spirit.

In all honesty, if I had my druthers, I'd probably be a vegetarian; in my heart of hearts, I love beef more than any other person. I ate a ton of barbecue the other night, but I knew that my body was really craving vegetables. I denied it, the barbecue was satisfying and wonderful, but I would have rather had one of the recipes from Franklin's book—I was reading it this morning and I came to the beet and avocado recipe; *this* is the kind of food I really want to eat. It really speaks to me. Like Franklin, I'm also really in love with grains of all types; I grew up eating couscous and all kinds of crazy stuff because my parents lived in Berkeley. I also absolutely love wild rice—and Franklin mentions wild rice and black quinoa in this book . . . so that really touched my soul. This is the kind of food I just love.

This is the kind of food I really want to eat; this is the kind of food I just love.

It's public knowledge that I've always wanted to open up a restaurant where I would serve my chicken with an array of roasted and raw vegetables, and carefully prepared different grains. Nothing from the wheat family, and no dairy or anything. I believe that Franklin really understands that sensibility. He also intuitively understands the importance of olive oil: Olive oil, I believe, is king. As an ingredient, it's an amazing piece of culinary history. And the fact that it's become so popular in America is so edifying. I knew way back when, when I discovered French olive oil, and then olive oil from Liguria, or Tuscany, or Central Greece, or Israel, that it's the greatest ingredient in the world. So to celebrate olive oil the way Franklin does is, to me, really almost everything in cooking.

> To celebrate olive oil the way Franklin does is, to me, really almost everything in cooking.

(Not that I don't love lard every once in a while—and I was the butter king for many years, and I love cream—but olive oil? I could just drink it.)

Franklin is primarily influenced by Mediterranean ingredients and style; he worked in Positano, at the famous Le Sirenuse, which is one of my favorite restaurants in the world; it's the sort of place that marries the rustic and the old fashioned with the modern. When I was there, I just didn't want to leave. When Franklin mentioned Positano in the book, it sort of clicked for me that this is

This is what Franklin's cookbook was about: It was about sunlight, it was about warm tomatoes off the vine, it was about picking olives and crushing them, it was about lemon and mint and all those great flavors that I just love about Italy, France, Tunisia, Israel, Greece. This is *really* the way I want to cook, and I want to eat.

what his cookbook is about: It was about sunlight, it was about warm tomatoes off the vine, it was about picking olives and crushing them, it was about lemon and mint and all those great flavors that I just love about Italy, France, Tunisia, Israel, Greece. This is *really* the way I want to cook, and I want to eat. Not that I don't love Chinese food or Thai food. But if I had to choose a setting—like Franklin really has for his food and his writing—it's the Mediterranean.

Franklin Becker also has a grasp of science, where other chefs do not; he was forced to. His son has autism, and he's devoted to trying to find ways to help him with food; this dedication to his son's health and wellness forced him to really explore every kind of culinary possibility both scientific and nutritional. To me, that's really cool; not too many chefs have the ability to do this. But Franklin does it without being pedantic. There's a lot of finger-wagging when it comes to the discussion about good, or wholesome, ingredients, which can take the pleasure out of it. I'm obviously from the Alice Waters school of food—find the best ingredients and try not to screw them up—and that's the school that Franklin comes from. He finds the best ingredients in the market, and then, thanks to his terrific improvisational ability, makes swaps as he needs to, and this is what he teaches his readers. If he doesn't find quinoa, he switches over to another grain. I really adore this about Franklin: He's a very technically savvy chef with the ability to perform, but he's also extremely flexible, and this comes through in this book. It's this combination that separates the chefs from the wannabes: They have that technical ability to

Franklin Becker also has a grasp of science, where other chefs do not; he was forced to. His son has autism, and he's devoted to trying to find ways to help him with food; this dedication to his son's health and wellness forced him to really explore every kind of culinary possibility both scientific and nutritional. Not too many chefs have the ability to do this. Franklin does it without being pedantic.

perform, but they can also make their food accessible for home cooks, and show them the way a chef might do it at home.

Franklin isn't satisfied with *just good enough*. You can taste all of the ingredients that he puts into his dishes, and you know what they're going to do to the recipe and the end result.

But Franklin Becker is also a nose-to-the-grindstone, wrestle-with-the-ingredients kind of chef, who gets them to do what he wants them to do. He has an intensity which I find really delightful and I think that's a huge part of his personality as a cook: He wants to get to the point where he's happy with his dishes, and that's, of course, what a great chef does. Franklin *owns* his dishes; there aren't a lot of people who do that. A lot of chefs just put ingredients together and it's "good enough"; Franklin isn't satisfied with *just good enough*. You can taste all of the ingredients that he puts into his dishes, and you know what they're going to do to the recipe and the end result. But he's also classically trained, and it comes through: Franklin veers to the rustic, but he also talks about making a mirepoix the right way, or dicing, slicing, or carving the right way, and that, too, is very helpful for the home cook. Understanding how to do these things offers home cooks *chef mojo,* and Franklin does that with finesse.

When I'm at home, I cook very simply; I'd rather have a squash blossom taco with a bit of avocado than anything else. These are the simple, healthy, delicious pleasures that I love; this is also the way Franklin Becker cooks, and what he's about.

Jonathan Waxman

Friendly Fat

For more years than most of us can remember, we have been bombarded with the gospel of low fat and even no fat, but the inescapable truth is fats are necessary for good health. Fat is one of the three nutrients that your body needs to keep the machine running: carbohydrates for quick energy, protein to build muscles and tissues, and fat for energy storage and smooth functioning of all of your vital organs. Every membrane of the billions and billions of cells in your body requires fat. Without it, you would just be a pile of organic molecules that couldn't communicate with each other, no smarter than a bathtub full of amoebas. In fact, the amoebas would probably win an IQ contest.

Humans have always prized fat in their diet both for its flavor and its energy. The question is not "Do you need fat?" You do. The real question is "What kind of fat and how much?" Here is where things become a little tricky and where, frankly, many of us—myself included—get mixed up. Part of the problem is the rivers of data and the oceans of opinions about what makes up a healthy diet versus an unhealthy one. If you try to keep up with the latest studies, you can wind up more baffled than when you started. As the great authority on nutrition Marion Nestle has said, "For every PhD there is an equal but opposite PhD."

One of the challenges in figuring out the proper role of fat is the word itself. When we say someone is fat, we usually mean they are overweight, and most scientists agree that being overweight is not healthy. Diabetes, heart disease, and cancer have been linked to too much weight. But being fat and eating fat are two different things. It is not only fat in our diet that accounts for the billions of pounds Americans have put on in recent decades. It is calories. To be sure, some calories come from fat, but the "Great Expansion" of the American waistline of the last 30 years happened at the same time that we have restricted our consumption of fats. Skim milk sippers and Snackwell snackers often compensated with carbs and protein, yet the obesity statistics went straight up. Why? Because we are eating more calories and many of those calories are from refined or processed foods like white bread, cereals with a lot of added sugar, and 32-ounce sodas. No matter where you get your calories from, if you eat more than you burn off each day, your body is going to store the excess as fat. Three thousand calories of eggplant, or millet, or ice cream will all have the same effect on your weight.

Although fat is essential, it is important to know that not all fats are created equal. While an ounce of butter and an ounce of olive oil have the same number of calories, their fats are very different. Butter is largely saturated fat—which is solid at room temperature—and olive oil is largely unsaturated fat—liquid at room temperature. The fat in nuts is mostly unsaturated, while the cheese on your pizza is full of saturated fat. Unsaturated fats don't clog up your arteries. Most evidence says that saturated fats can, although recently even that has been questioned by some scientists. There is a lot more to the science and chemistry of fats than one simple explanation. You can have your pick of thousands of academic papers on such topics as the nutritional value of omega-3 fatty acids and omega-6s—both of which should be included in any healthy diet—but the bottom line is, unsaturated fats from plants and seafood won't clog your arteries.

Most of my diet—and the great majority of recipes in this book—calls for unsaturated fats and a little of the saturated kind. (Have you ever met a chef who didn't like a pat of butter now and then?) All of the fats that I use are found in nature. One kind of fat that you will not find in this book—or in nature, for that matter—is trans fat, which is nothing more than vegetable oil that has been altered so that it is solid at room temperature. Some cooks use it because it never goes rancid, and it doesn't smoke at the higher temperatures that make crunchy chicken nuggets, popcorn shrimp, and golden french fries. But study after study shows a diet heavy in trans fats or saturated fats is downright unhealthy. You probably don't need all the extra calories, and your heart and arteries will be much happier with less of the kinds of fat that are linked to heart disease.

Fat makes so many things taste better. It creates that round, smooth sensation that we chefs call mouth feel. Sautéing in hot fat helps vegetables, meats, fish, and poultry develop a golden crust that greatly enhances flavor and texture. Salad becomes much more interesting with an oil-based dressing; without it, you'd have a boring plateful of raw greens. It's probably no coincidence that at the same time that oil in salad makes for a more pleasurable way to eat vegetables, it also pulls out vitamins, minerals, and nutrients that would pass straight through your body without doing you a bit of good if they weren't dissolved in oil. I say it's no coincidence because I am a great believer in the idea that food that is more naturally delicious is also more nutritious. Note that I said naturally delicious, not full of additives to pump up flavor. To my way of thinking, fat makes food dance; it brings a magical extra something that elevates the flavor of just about everything.

Learning to Cook for Health: My Long Journey

When I began my professional career, I was, like many young chefs, more interested in doing what the stars in the cooking world were doing than in evolving my own healthy style. It was the era of "Tall Food," more suited to architects or Lego masters than to cooks. Eventually I realized that kind of showy cooking wasn't me, and I expect it is not the way you cook either. Have you ever had dinner at a friend's home and he served you a dish that looked more like a 3-D food sculpture than a meal? I haven't. That's because real people don't cook or serve that way.

But there was something else happening in the food world at that time that was much more interesting to me. I got to work for chefs who were reinventing American food. Bobby Flay and David Walzog, two of my mentors (and employers), put the emphasis on big, bold flavors, rather than fancy arrangements and complicated sauces. They taught me about the flavors of the American Southwest: bright, aromatic, spicy, and most of all, fresh. You will find echoes of their way of thinking about food all through this book. And, because of them, you will also find a lot of avocados in these pages. I must have made a couple of tons of guacamole in those years, and that was before I knew that avocados are loaded with healthy fat.

Then in 1993 and 1994 two things happened that pushed me down the road to healthy food. One was a good thing, the other . . . not so good. If you had seen me at that time, you might not have recognized me. I weighed 235 pounds—way too much for good health. Apart from not liking the way I looked and felt carrying all that weight around, I had developed diabetes, a health issue that is all too common as more Americans eat themselves into obesity.

I had to change the way I ate. Good-bye pasta, pizza, white rice, that second glass of wine, ice cream, and chocolate. By cutting down on portions, eating less red meat and full-fat dairy, and consuming more fresh vegetables, I took off close to 30 pounds in less than 2 months. It was life changing and led to two cookbooks for diabetics (and for people interested in not ending up as diabetics). Healthy fat wasn't my focus yet, but I did have to consider how much fat was in my recipes because even healthy fat is loaded with calories.

Fresh from my run-in with obesity and diabetes, in the fall of 1994 I took a job at Le Sirenuse, a seaside restaurant in Positano, Italy, and began my love affair with olive oil. Although I have always been a fan of this miraculous food, I'd have to say that I became a true believer when I worked at Sirenuse. Those 6 months changed my life. What we did there was so simple; most of our

Okay, I Admit It, I Occasionally Eat Meat and Dairy

Seafood. Nuts. Avocados. Olive oil. Does this mean that I never eat meat, butter, or cheese? Heaven forbid! These can also be nutritious foods that are key to meeting many of the body's needs, and they are delicious; they're just not the mainstay of my diet, nor do I eat them in the giant portions that they serve at an NFL training table. A little goes a long way. The pleasure that you will get from eating these foods occasionally more than offsets the damage you'll do by stressing out when you constantly deny yourself.

Because of their diet, the meat of free-ranging, grass-fed animals is rich in antioxidants, vitamins, and minerals that are not found in the meat of animals that are confined to feed lots, pens, and cages (where they are fed corn, soybeans, and antibiotics). Animals that are raised out of doors and allowed to graze freely on the foods that nature intended them to eat produce fat that is higher in heart-healthy fatty acids. In fact, the farmers of Spain refer to their prized "black foot" pigs as "the four-footed olive tree," in recognition of the fact that their fat is high in the same heart-healthy monounsaturated fat as olives.

cooking was done on a wood-fired grill. The vegetables came from the garden, the meat from the local farms, and the fish straight out of the sea.

As I look back on it, it's clear that Positano made me a believer in the basic tenets of the Mediterranean diet: lots of vegetables and fresh fish, fewer and smaller portions of meat, and olive oil with everything, or so it seemed. Why so much olive oil? Because its mild, slightly floral, slightly earthy flavor never dominates. Instead, it helps simple, fresh foods sing. It highlights the intrinsic flavor of ingredients. Of course, for ingredients to express intrinsic flavor, they need to be at their peak, so a commitment to the Mediterranean diet brought with it an appreciation of local and seasonal produce. Ditto for free-range meat and poultry and sustainably harvested seafood. In the decades since the Mediterranean diet first attracted public attention, virtually every study has concluded that it contributes to health and longevity. It is no accident, then, that olive oil is among the healthiest of fats, and particularly high in monounsaturated fat, a proven artery cleaner. Much of this book represents my further explorations of the Mediterranean diet, sometimes combined with flavors of India, Asia, Mexico, the American Southwest, and my own obsession with thinking up new recipes 24/7.

Without my realizing it yet, my career as a chef was pointing me down the path of healthy fat: first in the avocados that characterized the Southwest food that I made in my early years and then in the olive oil that I came to rely on more and more after my return from Italy. It was then that another life-changing experience brought about more culinary exploration. My son, Sean, was born in 1999, and not long after we learned that he was afflicted with autism. Like many autistic kids, Sean did not tolerate gluten very well. Dairy was also a problem. In fact, it seemed that almost every food created a different and troublesome issue.

I thought if I could find the right diet, while it might not overcome autism, then at least it would make his life more comfortable. Because gluten definitely had a bad effect on him, I looked for substitutes. I discovered quinoa and buckwheat, two non-grains that taste like grains, satisfy the same craving, and combine with other ingredients in much the same way grain does. To replace the wheat flour that was now off-limits, I experimented with flours made with ground nuts. And if you are a chef, once you have a lot of nuts hanging around, you are going to find new ways to use them. I certainly did, especially in salads. Their crunch is pleasing. Their flavor is deep and earthy and enriches other ingredients. And the fats in almost all nuts are almost all monounsaturated or polyunsaturated; in other words, healthy fats.

I wish I could tell you that I found the magic key to Sean's food issues. I tried everything I could think of, but nothing worked. Still it is that little boy whom I have to thank for opening my eyes to non-gluten ingredients, to natural dairy substitutes, and the deliciousness, versatility, and healthy attributes of nuts.

So from my beginnings as a cook, seduced by the flavors of the Southwest, to my becoming a pilgrim to Italy, the land of recipes driven by simple ingredients (and lots of olive oil), then a diabetic who needed to reform his diet, then a New York chef trying to find a way to help his son eat more happily, I found myself bumping into healthy fats. This book is the result of that interesting journey, one that I could never have predicted when I got my cooking school diploma in 1993, but one that has allowed me to develop a delicious and healthy way of eating.

My Favorite Healthy Fats

Olive Oil

I use olive oil more often than any other fat. It adds delicate flavor, aroma, and texture to nearly every ingredient that you combine it with. If it were in a movie, I would give it the award for Best Supporting Ingredient. In a salad, olive oil pulls nutrients out of raw vegetables that would otherwise be lost. It adds body and smoothness as a finishing touch to soups and cooked vegetables. As a medium for sautéing, unlike butter, it doesn't take over. However, like butter, it has a low smoke point, so for aggressive frying at high heat, I might choose another healthy oil such as canola or safflower. But for day-to-day all-around flavor and versatility, olive oil rules.

Avocados

If olive oil is the Best Supporting Ingredient, then I would have to say that the overall star of the healthy fat world is the avocado. In my early restaurant years, a large part of every day was devoted to peeling avocados, scooping out the smooth flesh, and making more guacamole than anyone had ever made in the whole history of the world . . . or at least it seemed that way to me. Hey, people needed something to put on those chips that they nibbled on while drinking highly profitable margaritas. What lifts the avocado in my esteem is its silky smooth mouth feel: almost like a perfectly churned ice cream. I often use it as a substitute for butter or other oils when I want to enrich a recipe. If you blend it really well, you can use it wherever a recipe calls for mayonnaise. Avocados are loaded with heart-healthy monounsaturated fat and packed with antioxidants.

In writing my diabetes cookbooks (*The Diabetic Chef* and *Eat & Beat Diabetes with Picture Perfect Weight Loss*), I found that avocados could actually help lower insulin resistance.

Nuts

I have eaten nuts my whole life, but, as I mentioned earlier, I got serious about cooking with nuts when I began to research healthy recipes that my son could—and would—eat. At that time, I came across an eating plan known as the Specific Carbohydrate Diet. It was developed by Elaine Gottschall, a biologist who successfully relieved her daughter's colitis by cutting out gluten, sugar, and dairy. It was recommended for autism sufferers, who often have a problem with these three foods. Nuts, however, were fine. I began to cook with nuts, using them in flours, as fillers, as accents in salads, or with cooked vegetables.

All nuts have fat, and their oils brim with elegant, powerful, toasty flavor; they provide little islands of texture and taste in everything they're added to. The fat in many nuts such as walnuts and pistachios has also been shown to actually lower LDL, the so-called bad cholesterol. Because nuts contain so much good fat, protein, and carbs, they are also high in calories. But if you think you need to avoid them in order to keep your weight under control, surprisingly, the opposite is true: The dense calories of nuts actually make you feel fuller faster. (The scientific term for this feeling of fullness is *satiety,* which rhymes with "society.") Where nuts are concerned, a little goes a long way, and they can actually help you maintain or lose weight. Nuts helped me control my weight when I was diagnosed with diabetes.

Seafood

Fish and shellfish are excellent sources of protein; the big difference between them and land-dwelling animals is that the fats in fish are typically very heart healthy. Some of my favorite fish, such as tuna, salmon, the often overlooked mackerel, and the lowly but delicious sardine, are great sources of omega-3s, which are critical to keep your arteries clean and free-flowing. I am careful about which fish I eat because it is well known that we have been overexploiting our ocean resources, endangering many species. Always double-check that the fish you plan on eating is sustainably harvested. A number of organizations publish wallet cards and apps that can help you keep track of which species get the green light.

My Goal: Creating Healthy Flavors That Pop

If you look at a lot of healthy eating cookbooks, they are all about what you shouldn't eat: no carbs, no sugar, no fat, no dairy. Being told what you can't eat is no way to kick-start your palate and send you to the kitchen to try recipes that make you really salivate. So from the outset, this is a "Do" cookbook rather than a "Don't" cookbook.

This is the perspective I cook from: I know that healthy fats are good for you. I also know that many of you are vegans, vegetarians, and possibly gluten-free and lactose intolerant. The great majority of recipes in this book meet all of those standards. I have also included a few meat recipes, but not of the 2-pound beefsteak variety. Some recipes call for yogurtlike kefir or ricotta cheese or a pat of butter. A handful include wheat. And there's a bunch based on seafood, which, as I've said above, is a great source of healthy fat. But the lion's share are VVNGND (Vegan, Vegetarian, Non-Gluten, Non-Dairy).

In writing this book, I took it as a challenge to create great-tasting recipes for the home chef. Thirty years in restaurant kitchens, many of them working with some of the most creative and consistently mind-blowing chefs, have taught me a thing or two about making food that jumps off the plate. I have learned that there is no such thing as a boring ingredient. Recipes can be boring. Chefs can be uninspired. But it is my rock-solid belief that every ingredient can be made part of a delicious recipe. It is up to the cook—you and me—to make flavor that pops. By that I mean, you can truly taste every ingredient. For sure, there are many great recipes in this world that combine and marry flavors until you can't quite put your finger on what it is that you taste. That's not what I do. I look for that wonderful something that wakes up your palate and makes you take notice in a way that says, "Hey, this string bean (or beet, or whiff of thyme, or piece of salmon) is terrific!"

When I say that every ingredient can be made delicious, what I mean is that every great ingredient has this potential. Produce needs to be fresh and in season. I don't much care for oranges in July or tomatoes in January. Sometimes, amid all the beautiful, hard-to-make dishes we see on food television and in magazines, we forget that it all starts with great ingredients. To this day, the restaurant review that I treasure the most—and I have received my share of nice ones—came from Bill Grimes, who was, at that time, the restaurant critic of the *New York Times.* In his review of Local, a restaurant in the theater district where

I was chef in 1999, Grimes wrote, "He knows how to shop. The beans don't just sit there emanating greenness; they come loaded with bean flavor." That part about knowing how to shop really pleased me.

Consider that fresh green bean that the *Times* singled out. If you cook a green bean, it should always be a fresh one, in season, and probably local because only then will it be at its peak of flavor. You will have to do less to it to make it taste great. In cooking, as with so many creative pursuits, less is often more. So before I make up a recipe, I think long and hard about that bean, or any ingredient for that matter. Your goal, always, is to achieve the maximum of flavor and pleasure. Too many people, including many viewers of food television, think of cooking as a competition and the more complicated the recipe, the better the chef. But in my mind the simple art of roasting vegetables well is a lot more impressive than being able to dice vegetables into teeny tiny squares and creating artsy compositions on a plate.

In writing this book, just as I do whenever I go shopping for ingredients or before I start to create a recipe, the first thing I asked myself was, "Why do I want to eat a particular thing?" It used to be that the only answer I was looking for was good taste. That still is the measure by which a recipe rises or falls. But now, I also need to know what effect different foods will have on my health, my family's health, your health.

A Cookbook for the Way We Eat Today

As you look through my recipes, you'll notice right off the bat that the portions are not huge. There are a few reasons for this. First, there is no question that one of the major drivers of the increase in obesity is the size of portions. We fill our plates with much more food than our grandparents did and much more food than the rest of the world does. If you don't believe me, just compare the average size of a pasta order in America with what they eat in Italy, the homeland of great pasta. Chances are your single bowl of spaghetti in New York, Cleveland, or Seattle would be enough for three orders in Rome. All those extra calories add up, and the end result is more weight and more body fat.

Smaller portions don't mean, however, that I want you to get up from the table hungry. I have found, in recent years, that my customers are more likely to share different dishes than to stick to an attitude of "I ordered this and you ordered that, so finish your plate and I'll finish mine." These days, most people like to mix and match, exploring different flavors and textures. You'll see that many of these recipes call for portion sizes that allow you to graze instead of gobble. And since many can be made in advance, you don't always have to prepare a multicourse meal from scratch in order to enjoy a little variety at the table. If you do mix and match, though, don't feel you have to finish everything. Leftovers are one of the greatest answers to the riddle "I don't feel like cooking today, so what can I eat?" Leftovers have often been the running start I needed to go on and create many new recipes.

This book started with a health question. How can I create recipes that will deliver flavor and nutrition that is both healthy and pleasing? Once I narrowed down the fats, cut down on gluten, and included a number of vegan options, I jumped into the fun part of writing a cookbook . . . cooking.

Franklin Becker

My Go-To Ingredients

As you will see in my recipes, my goal, always, is to maximize flavor. Simple, but important foods that I cook with time and again, such as grains, beans, and vegetables, really benefit from tried and true (or, as I like to say, "Beckered and Blessed") combinations of spices, herbs, and other seasonings that have the ability to complement and bump up particular flavor profiles. Because I don't always know what I am going to find in the markets where I do my shopping, I always make sure to keep my pantry well stocked with herbs, spices, aromatics, seasonings, sweeteners, and other flavor boosters and pick-me-ups so that no matter what I am cooking I know I can make a delicious, healthy fat meal packed with flavor.

Spices and Aromatics That Sweeten

Some spices have the ability to nudge the most flavor out of sweet ingredients. It's not that they make the ingredients they're cooked with sweeter, per se, nor are the spices themselves sweet. Instead they provide the proper flavor background to showcase all the sweetness in everything from onions, to nuts, to shrimp.

Black cardamom pods	Cloves, whole	Nutmeg, whole
Green cardamom, whole	Ginger (whole fresh)	Vanilla (bean)
Cinnamon	Mace, whole blade (not used in book)	Star anise

Spices That Heat

Spicy, hot ingredients wake up our sensitive taste receptors and, in so doing, make our taste buds tingle, amplifying flavor. Think of them as a wake-up call for your palate. Even if you don't like spicy food, a little heat goes a long way in rounding out and intensifying flavor .

Black pepper

Red-pepper flakes

Cayenne pepper

Piri piri (African bird's-eye chile pepper; very hot)

Gochutgaru (Korean chili powder; very hot)

Paprika

Pimenton (smoky Spanish paprika)

Spices That Accent

Some aromatic spices provide an accent to the natural flavors in other ingredients. Like a flute in an orchestra that provides a high note to the bottom bass section, these accents often strike solo notes that draw you in to deeper layers of gustatory, sensual experience. For example, sumac provides a high, sour note to more mellow flavors; fenugreek provides a natural earthiness, as does cumin, which, when toasted, also adds a bit of smoke.

Sumac

Fenugreek

Coriander seed

Cumin seed

Mustard seed

Herbs and Aromatics for Savoriness

Fresh herbs add depth of flavor and earthy green freshness. Sometimes I let them cook long and slow, in long-simmering bean dishes and vegetable stews. When added to recipes at the last minute, their volatile oils carry a tantalizing aroma that makes you jump out of your seat with anticipation when they arrive as a garnish on a pork chop or a just-off-the-grill steak.

Basil	Rosemary	Cilantro
Bay leaf	Parsley	Chives
Mint	Tarragon	Oregano
Thyme	Chervil	Shiso
Sage	Dill	

Acids to Provide Tartness

Acids brighten and raise all the flavors in a dish, and balance sweetness and saltiness. They make heavy dishes lighter tasting and make sauces pop with flavor.

Apple cider vinegar	White balsamic vinegar	Limes
Red wine vinegar	Sherry vinegar	Oranges
Rice wine vinegar	Lemons	

Must-Have Spice Blends

As I travel the world, I am always struck by the way that different cultures rely on certain combinations and marriages of spices that give an underlying, instantly recognizable theme to a regional cuisine. These are natural "flavor partners" that have evolved over the centuries not only because they taste great, but because they are specific to a geographical region and culture.

Madras curry—an Indian spice blend of fennel seeds, cumin, mustard seeds, coriander, cinnamon, pepper, nutmeg, cloves, cardamom, turmeric, ginger, and cayenne.

Garam masala—less assertive than Madras curry, this Indian spice blend features turmeric, black and white pepper, cloves, cinnamon, cumin, and cardamom.

Pickling spice—used to make pickles on New York's Lower East Side back in the day. Usually a combination of mustard seed, allspice, cinnamon, clove, coriander, red pepper, ginger, and bay leaf, pickling spice pairs well with tart and salty brines for everything from meats to vegetables. I love it with meat, poultry, and fish.

Zatarain's Crawfish, Shrimp & Crab Boil—believe it or not, this New Orleans spice blend company started out as makers of root beer: This spice blend, which is available at most good supermarkets, is used for seafood boils and makes shrimp, crawfish, lobster, and crabs all explode with flavor: It contains mustard seed, coriander seed, allspice, bay leaf, black pepper, sugar, paprika, salt, and chile pepper.

My Favorite Flavor Bombs

Regional flavoring blends are not confined to herbs and spices. Many cultures take this and that—herbs, sauces, aromatics—from the whole larder to create combinations that lend a distinctive stamp to their cuisines. I came up with some of these on my own to give a distinctive flavor to my cuisine (I hope).

Asian—scallions, garlic, ginger, and soy sauce (tamari).

Mediterranean All-Stars—basil, mint, parsley.

Greek—oregano, red wine vinegar, and olive oil.

Italian—basil, parsley, garlic, onions, olive oil, perfect for red sauces.

Mushrooms and curry—a hint of curry brings out the *umami* in mushrooms. It boosts flavor like MSG—monosodium glutamate, a preservative and flavor "booster"— without adding store-bought MSG.

Oranges and olives—sweet oranges enhance the fruity saltiness of olives.

Cinnamon and thyme—earthy and sweet, this is a great (and unexpected) combination in desserts and savory applications.

Basil and cloves—their sweet, almost anise-y flavors complement each other.

Strawberries and beans (especially favas)—a combination of grassy and floral notes with fruitiness notes.

Salmon and fennel—Scandinavians wouldn't think of using anything but dill with their precious salmon, but I love the pairing of this rich fish with the sweet licorice notes of fennel.

Chicken with parsely, basil, and bay leaf—an unusual combination, but I find these herbs complement the gentle flavors of poultry rather than overpowering them the way that rosemary or thyme might.

Eggs and chervil, parsley, and tarragon or eggs with oregano— these herbs take the broad, mildly sulfuric flavor of eggs and add just enough herbal and floral notes to create depth and interest.

Chile peppers with chocolate and vanilla—this sweet and spicy combination was prized by Aztec emperors. Once you taste it, you'll know why.

Sweet and sour—the combination of these tastes is common to many national cuisines. My favorite is lemon, oranges, and honey.

Sweet and salty—any nut with sugar and sea salt. In for one, in for a handful. They are irresistible.

Ginger + garlic + chiles + lime + fish sauce—an amazing flavor combo that explodes on the palate. This is traditionally Thai and Vietnamese in influence.

Oils for Healthy Fat

For cooking, for adding flavor, and for round, satisfying mouth feel without the heaviness of saturated fats:

Canola oil	Safflower oil	Sesame oil, toasted
Olive oil	Hemp oil	

Salts for Seasoning

Used judiciously, salt elevates every element of taste and flavor; I couldn't cook without it. I like the consistency and flavor of kosher salt and the crunch of flaky sea salt.

Kosher salt

Flaky sea salt, like Maldon

Nuts and Seeds for Protein, Healthy Fat, and Texture

Nuts are packed with protein, their taste is sublime, and they provide a wonderful crunchy counterpoint in grain and vegetable dishes. Best of all, of course, is the fact that the fat in most nuts is healthy. You'll find them all through this book. Here are some of my favorite combinations.

Cashews are great with garlic and have a creamy texture.

Pistachios pair well with basil and parsley.

Walnuts go nicely with apples and dried fruits.

Almonds are the right partner for cauliflower.

Hazelnuts are good with chocolate or with mild ham (such as Spanish, Italian, and country ham).

Pecans are actually a fruit. This distinctly American nut is terrific with wild rice, brown rice, and apricots.

Peanuts make Thai food come alive with texture and taste.

Pine nuts are perfect for pesto with basil, parsley, and Parmesan cheese.

Pumpkin seeds are delicious toasted and tossed with Pecorino cheese and currants.

Sesame seeds are wonderful with Asian ingredients as well as Middle Eastern dishes.

Beans and Grains for Protein, Whole Carbohydrates, and Healthy Fat

Beans and many grains are excellent sources of protein, complex carbs, and fiber. On their own they can often be bland, but when prepared with almost any of the previous flavor boosters, they form the backbone of many of my recipes.

Chickpeas	Quinoa	Kasha
Lentils	Puffed millet	Rice
Great Northern white beans	Buckwheat soba	

For Pure Sweetness

Most of us like sweet flavor, but we all could do with less refined cane sugar. Here are my favorite sweeteners; I use them regularly and often in surprising applications.

Honey	Maple syrup	Currants
Agave	Maple sugar	Dates
Acacia honey	Coconut sugar	Raisins

CHAPTER 1

SALADS

Salads are all about texture and crunch in particular, which is why raw vegetables are so fundamental to them. The health bonus here is that raw vegetables have not lost any of their vitamins and minerals through cooking. As I mentioned earlier, fat is needed in order for your body to be able to make use of the vitamins and minerals in raw vegetables. I don't confine my salads to raw vegetables, though. I'll often throw in some cooked vegetables, nuts, cheese, or grains for contrasting textures because contrast always makes a recipe more interesting. Salads also need some acidity or tanginess to brighten up your palate, so vinegar, lemon juice, and even fresh fruits come into play. The great unifier that carries flavor from one bite to the next is healthy fat. It takes the many parts of a salad and unites them into a whole.

Beets, Goat Cheese, and Crunchy Herb Salad | 3

Baby Beets with Goat Cheese and Fennel | 5

Beets with Avocado and Kefir | 6

Tons of Crunch Summer Bean Salad | 7

Heirloom Tomatoes, Avocado, Mango, and Cucumber | 8

Strawberries, Fennel, and Cucumber Salad | 11

Autumn on a Plate | 12

Kale Salad with Pecorino Cheese, Pumpkin Seeds, and Grapes | 15

Lentils, Avocado, Oranges, Pecans, and Kale with Ginger Dressing | 16

Fresh Ricotta with Figs, Olive Oil, and Chili Flakes | 20

Radish, Apple, Hazelnut, and Arugula Salad | 21

Beets, Goat Cheese, and Crunchy Herb Salad

Beets and goat cheese go together like peanut butter and jelly. In this recipe, I give the combo added zip with a flavorful honey mustard vinaigrette. The icing on the cake, in a manner of speaking, is my take on gremolata. I took some liberties and added my own favorite combination of herbs and included orange zest because its fruity tanginess balances the alkaline beets.

serves 4

for the beets:

½ pound baby golden beets

4 tablespoons extra virgin olive oil, divided

Salt and fresh ground black pepper to taste

½ pound baby red beets

for the dressing:

3 tablespoons extra virgin olive oil

1 tablespoon sherry vinegar

1 tablespoon honey

1 teaspoon Dijon mustard

¼ pound baby candy striped beets, peeled and thinly sliced on a mandoline

for the gremolata:

3 tablespoons sunflower seeds, toasted

1 tablespoon chopped Italian parsley leaves

1 tablespoon chopped dill

1 tablespoon chopped mint leaves

1 tablespoon chopped chervil

1 teaspoon grated lemon zest

1 teaspoon grated orange zest

1 tablespoon extra virgin olive oil

2 teaspoons flaky sea salt

¼ teaspoon cayenne pepper

Salt and fresh ground black pepper to taste

to assemble:

4 ounces goat cheese, crumbled

to make the beets:

Preheat the oven to 350°F. On a piece of foil, toss the golden beets with 2 tablespoons of the olive oil, salt, and pepper and wrap tightly. Repeat with the red beets, the remaining 2 tablespoons olive oil, and a second piece of foil. Roast in the oven until fork-tender, about 30 minutes. Remove from the oven and peel the beets under cool running water while they're still hot.

to make the dressing:

Meanwhile, in a small bowl, whisk together the olive oil, sherry vinegar, honey, and mustard. Quarter the beets and place them in separate bowls. Pour half of the vinaigrette over each and toss. Marinate for 1 hour at room temperature. Place the striped beets in a third bowl.

to make the gremolata:

In a small bowl, combine the sunflower seeds, parsley, dill, mint, chervil, lemon zest, orange zest, olive oil, sea salt, and cayenne pepper. Divide among the beets, including the shaved beets, and toss. Season to taste with salt and pepper. Divide the beets among 4 plates. Top with the goat cheese and serve.

Baby Beets with Goat Cheese and Fennel

I love beets. You would kind of guess that from a guy who named his restaurant The Little Beet. Here, I combine beets—richly purple and deeply golden—with crisp, paper-thin shaved fennel, goat cheese, mint, and dill. The crunchy fennel adds snap, but just as important, its light licorice flavor brings out the sweetness of the beets. Mint does too. That makes them ideal partners for beets, which are known for their sugar content. This is a great winter salad because the colors and textures make it feel fresh as a spring breeze.

serves 4

for the beets:

- ½ pound baby golden beets
- 4 tablespoons extra virgin olive oil, divided
    Salt and fresh ground black pepper to taste
- ½ pound baby red beets

for the dressing:

- 3 tablespoons extra virgin olive oil
- 1 tablespoon sherry vinegar
- 1 tablespoon honey
- 1 teaspoon Dijon mustard
    Salt and fresh ground black pepper to taste

to assemble:

- ¼ pound baby candy striped beets, peeled and thinly sliced on a mandoline
- 1 grapefruit-size bulb fennel, trimmed, cored, and thinly shaved on a mandoline
    Juice of ½ lemon
- 1 tablespoon extra virgin olive oil
- 10 mint leaves, thinly sliced
- 2 sprigs dill, picked
    Salt and fresh ground black pepper to taste
- 2 ounces goat cheese, crumbled

to make the beets:

Preheat the oven to 350°F. On a piece of foil, toss the golden beets with 2 tablespoons of the olive oil, salt, and pepper and wrap tightly. Repeat with the red beets, the remaining 2 tablespoons olive oil, and a second piece of foil. Roast in the oven until fork-tender, about 30 minutes. Remove from the oven and peel the beets under cool running water while they're still hot.

to make the dressing:

Meanwhile, in a small bowl, whisk together the olive oil, sherry vinegar, honey, and mustard. Season to taste with salt and pepper. Quarter the beets and place them in separate bowls. Pour half of the vinaigrette over each and toss. Marinate for 1 hour at room temperature.

to assemble:

Place the striped beets and fennel in a medium bowl. In a small bowl, whisk together the lemon juice, olive oil, mint, and dill. Pour over the fennel and toss. Season with salt and pepper.

To serve, divide the fennel among 4 plates. Arrange some of each beet over the fennel and top with the goat cheese.

Beets with Avocado and Kefir

The pourable yogurt known as kefir has a beautiful consistency—similar to ranch dressing. That makes it a good match for beets because, as I mentioned before, beets are alkaline: the opposite of sour or acidic. That means they cry out for some tang. Kefir, like all yogurts, has the lactic acid that will satisfy that craving. Since kefir comes from the Middle East, it feels quite at home with aromatic spices such as cumin and coriander and a nice bunch of freshly picked herbs. Apparently, they never thought of pairing beets with avocados in the Middle East, probably because avocados are most definitely a New World fruit. But like many marriages between cultures, the result is quite beautiful. The added omega-3s and omega-6s in the kefir are an additional health benefit.

serves 4

½ pound red beets

½ pound golden beets

2 bay leaves

2 sprigs thyme

2 cloves garlic

2 tablespoons salt

3 ounces fresh squeezed orange juice

1 tablespoon white balsamic vinegar

3 tablespoons extra virgin olive oil

   Salt and fresh ground black pepper to taste

3 ounces kefir

¼ teaspoon coriander seeds, ground

¼ teaspoon cumin seeds, ground

   Zest of ¼ lemon

1 medium avocado

1 teaspoon chopped parsley

1 teaspoon chopped mint

Place the beets in 2 separate pots and fill with water to cover. Divide the bay leaves, thyme sprigs, garlic, and salt between the pots. Bring to a boil. Reduce the heat and bring to a simmer. Cook until the beets are fork-tender, about 30 minutes. (The smaller the beets, the quicker they will cook.) Let the beets cool in the water. Drain, removing and discarding the bay leaves, thyme, and garlic. Peel the beets, cut into ½-inch dice, and place in separate bowls.

In a small bowl, whisk together the orange juice, balsamic vinegar, olive oil, and salt and pepper to taste. Divide among the beets, toss to coat, and marinate in the refrigerator overnight.

In a small bowl, whisk together the kefir with the coriander, cumin, lemon zest, and salt and pepper to taste. Set aside.

Just before serving, cut the avocado into ½-inch dice, divide between the beets, and toss. Drizzle the kefir on each of 4 plates. Top with each of the beet mixtures, garnish with the parsley and mint, and serve chilled or at room temperature.

Tons of Crunch Summer Bean Salad

Whenever I see more than one kind of bean (shell beans or green beans) in a salad, I think of those tired old three-bean salads that take up space on a buffet without adding much interesting flavor or texture. Don't blame the beans. When you cut them into small dice and dress them with fresh herbs, olive oil, and lemon, they are a wake-up call for your palate. Here I use wax beans and green beans. Why this combination? Because that's what they had at the farmers' market the week that I first threw this together, and you can't do better than fresh produce in the height of the season. If sweet sugar snaps and dragon tongue (gotta love that name!) are available, use them. If tomatoes are happening, you could dice a nice juicy beefsteak, and while you're at it, crumble a little feta cheese on top. The salad can be made ahead and refrigerated. Serve at room temperature.

serves 4

---

1 pound mixed fresh yellow wax and string beans, cut into small dice

3 sprigs fresh mint, leaves only

2 sprigs fresh tarragon, leaves only

3 sprigs fresh parsley, leaves only

2 sprigs fresh dill, leaves only

Juice of 1 lemon (about 3 tablespoons)

2 tablespoons extra virgin olive oil

Sea salt and fresh ground black pepper to taste

In a medium bowl, combine the beans. Add the mint, tarragon, parsley, and dill and toss. Pour the lemon juice and olive oil over the bean mixture and toss to coat. Season with salt and pepper and serve.

Heirloom Tomatoes, Avocado, Mango, and Cucumber

On a hot summer afternoon, when lunch on a shady porch is as much activity as you can muster, this cool, sweet, crunchy salad is like air conditioning for your mouth (and soul): It's supremely soothing. It is naturally colorful and even prettier and more delicious with some herbs just snipped from your garden or, if you are a city dweller, from your windowsill flower pot. (You do have one, don't you? Everyone should always have some fresh herbs handy . . . no prior gardening experience needed.) Note that I call for English cucumber, which has very small seeds and is usually thinner than a regular cuke. Many supermarkets sell them these days. If you can't find them, get regular cukes.

serves 4

---

1 medium avocado

1 pint heirloom cherry tomatoes, halved

1 medium mango, cut into ½-inch dice

1 English cucumber, seeded and cut into ½-inch dice

6 tablespoons extra virgin olive oil

2 tablespoons white balsamic vinegar

Juice of ½ lemon (about 2 tablespoons)

1 teaspoon fresh mint, finely chopped

1 teaspoon fresh basil, finely chopped

1 teaspoon Italian parsley, finely chopped

Salt and fresh ground black pepper to taste

Just before serving, cut the avocado into ½-inch dice. In a medium bowl, combine the tomatoes, avocado, mango, cucumber, olive oil, vinegar, lemon juice, mint, basil, and parsley. Toss to coat all of the ingredients. Season with salt and pepper to taste. Serve at room temperature.

Strawberries, Fennel, and Cucumber Salad

While traveling down South with my son, he requested a stop at Cracker Barrel for their mashed potatoes (which he is wild about). They had a salad that day of strawberries and cucumbers. It surprised the heck out of me, but the proof is always in the eating, and the combination of crunch and sweetness was terrific. When I got back to New York, I played around with this unlikely combination. Basil and fennel boost the fresh flavor and crisp texture here. I'm fond of a glass of wheat beer to wash this down, but there's nothing wrong with Pinot Grigio or a Cheval—both wines that are just as crisp as the fennel and cukes.

serves 4

---

1 pint small strawberries, rinsed, hulled, and cut in half lengthwise

½ pound fennel, thinly sliced on a mandoline

1 whole English cucumber, peel on, thinly sliced on a mandoline

½ cup basil, leaves only

2 tablespoons extra virgin olive oil

1 tablespoon white balsamic vinegar

Salt and fresh ground black pepper to taste

In a medium bowl, combine the strawberries, fennel, cucumber, basil, olive oil, and vinegar. Toss to coat. Season with salt and pepper and serve chilled.

Autumn on a Plate

This is a salad completely made with the harvest of the fall. It is so flavorful that I think it can go head-to-head with any summer salad. I first made it for a charity benefit at the Center for Discovery, which works with special needs children and adults in a country farm setting. It was a sit-down dinner for 275, and I had the farm as my supermarket. Instead of aisles, there were lush rows of vegetables and orchards to stroll. This was the shortest farm-to-table commute that any vegetable could take. Don't be put off by the number of ingredients. For some reason, people won't complain about having lots of ingredients if you are talking about paella or bouillabaisse, but they expect their vegetable recipes to be much simpler. Not me. I think vegetables can be as complex and want just as much care and thought as any lobster, beef, or poultry recipe.

serves 4

for the squash:

- 1 pound kabocha squash, halved lengthwise and seeded
- Salt and fresh ground black pepper to taste
- 1 tablespoon extra virgin olive oil
- 1 tablespoon light brown sugar
- 1 cup water

for the vinaigrette:

- 1 small leek, white part only, thinly sliced
- 1 tablespoon Dijon mustard
- 6 tablespoons olive oil
- 2 tablespoons honey
- 2 tablespoons lemon juice
- 2 tablespoons sherry vinegar
- 1 teaspoon whole tarragon leaves
- Salt and fresh ground black pepper to taste

for the salad:

- 1/2 pound mustard greens, rinsed and stems removed
- 1/2 pound Brussels sprouts, tough outer leaves removed, stem ends trimmed, and thinly shaved on a mandoline
- 1 small watermelon radish, thinly sliced
- 1 medium Gala apple, cored, thinly sliced
- 1 small grapefruit-size celery root, peeled and diced
- 1/2 cup blanched skinless hazelnuts, toasted
- 1 ounce Parmigiano-Reggiano, shaved
- Salt and fresh ground black pepper to taste

to make the squash:

Preheat the oven to 400°F. Season the squash halves with salt and pepper, drizzle with the olive oil, and sprinkle with brown sugar. Pour the water in a baking pan and add the squash, flesh side down. Roast until fork-tender, about 30 minutes, and let cool. Peel and cut into 1/2-inch dice and set aside.

to make the vinaigrette:

In a medium bowl, whisk together the leek, mustard, olive oil, honey, lemon juice, vinegar, and tarragon leaves. Season to taste with salt and pepper.

to make the salad:

In a large bowl, combine the mustard greens, Brussels sprouts, radish, apple, celery root, hazelnuts, and cheese. Add the squash and toss with the vinaigrette. Season to taste with salt and pepper. Serve chilled.

Kale Salad with Pecorino Cheese, Pumpkin Seeds, and Grapes

While kale salads have gained tremendous popularity in recent years, there's no getting around the fact that kale is often quite tough and hard to chew. One solution for you kale lovers is to use baby kale. It's so tender, even the fibrous stems go down easily. I have made this salad with pickled currants for a long time, and judging from their orders, my customers keep coming back for it. I thought that the burst of sweet, juicy flavor and soft texture of ripe grapes would work nicely. For crunch, some toasted pumpkin seeds make for good texture contrast. The sweet and sour dressing partners well with Pecorino, which is more tart and pungent than the more common dusting of Parmigiano.

If you don't have fresh grapes, then dried currants or raisins will do. Soak the currants or raisins in water or vinegar till they plump up.

serves 4

---

1 pound baby kale, rinsed

1 tablespoon pumpkin seeds, toasted

¼ cup halved red or white grapes

Juice of 2 lemons (about 6 tablespoons)

2 teaspoons honey

4 tablespoons extra virgin olive oil

Salt and fresh ground black pepper to taste

2 tablespoons grated Pecorino cheese

In a salad bowl, combine the kale, pumpkin seeds, and grapes and toss.

In a small bowl, whisk together the lemon, honey, and olive oil. Season with salt and pepper. Pour over the kale mixture and toss to coat. Sprinkle the cheese over and serve immediately.

Lentils, Avocado, Oranges, Pecans, and Kale with Ginger Dressing

If I ever took this off the menu at my Manhattan restaurant, Little Beet, there would be a lot of long faces. It all started with a meal I had at Public, a great restaurant in the East Village. Before then, I had never given much thought to cold or room temperature lentils, but the wonderful chef Brad Farmerie made an insanely flavorful lentil dish. I realized that, as with so many healthful ingredients, if you add bright flavors, it really wakes them up. Here you get a big citrus burst from the orange and lushness from the avocado. If you are not yet convinced that lentils can be more than *meh*, once you try this, you will agree I am not overselling. This is a keeper.

serves 4

for the lentils:

¼ cup finely diced onion

1 tablespoon canola oil

1 cup green lentils, picked over and rinsed

1 clove garlic

1 bay leaf

2 cups water

2 teaspoons salt

for the salad:

1 avocado, cut into ½-inch dice

1 medium orange, sectioned

3 tablespoons pecan halves, toasted

4 ounces baby kale, whole leaves

2 tablespoons parsley leaves

Grated zest and juice of 1 lemon (about 3 tablespoons juice)

½ cup canola oil or grapeseed oil

2 tablespoons ginger juice

2 tablespoons honey

Salt and fresh ground black pepper to taste

to make the lentils:

In a medium pot over low heat, combine the onion and oil and sweat until translucent, about 5 minutes. Add the lentils and stir to coat with the oil. Cook for 5 minutes. Add the garlic, bay leaf, and water, cover, and simmer for 20 minutes. Add the salt and simmer for 10 minutes. Drain and discard the bay leaf and garlic. Place the cooked lentils on a baking sheet and allow to cool to room temperature.

to make the salad:

In a serving bowl, combine the cooked lentils, avocado, orange, and pecans and lightly toss. Add the kale, parsley, and lemon zest. In a small bowl, whisk together the lemon juice, oil, ginger juice, and honey. Season with salt and pepper. Pour over the lentil mixture and toss to coat. Serve at room temperature.

How to Make Ginger Juice

Peel a piece of fresh ginger and grate it into a bowl. Wrap the grated ginger in a piece of cheesecloth and squeeze the juice back into the bowl.

Fresh Ricotta with Figs,
Olive Oil, and Chili Flakes

Fresh Ricotta with Figs, Olive Oil, and Chili Flakes

We all have heard a lot about farm-to-table, but how about cow-to-table? My girlfriend Cindy and I were on a visit to Sorrento, a picture-postcard town overlooking the Bay of Naples. There, in the rich soil of Campania, the Marciano family welcomes visitors to the farm that has been in their family for generations. Lemons, limes, and walnuts all grow on the rolling acres where happy cows—or at least they looked happy to me—graze on the sweet grass. This was the first time that a visit to a restaurant started with the owners asking me to milk a cow! Well, when in Rome (or in this case Sorrento). . . . So I followed orders and we made fresh burrata, mozzarella, and ricotta before heading up to the farmhouse, where our hosts fed us a meal I will never forget. We started off with some prosciutto, peppers, mozzarella, and olives. Then we were served ricotta topped with chili flakes and olive oil, and some crusty bread followed by penne with sausage and red sauce. The meal ended with lemon ricotta cheesecake and some limoncello. It was all super, but then, what meal isn't in Italy? However, because I had a hand in making it, I will always remember the simple, spicy, creamy, chunky ricotta, with a lashing of olive oil and a sprinkling of red-pepper flakes. For my own version, I tore up some figs and added them for sweetness and chewiness. Freshly made cheeses, such as mozzarella and ricotta, have less butterfat by volume than aged cheeses, where the fat concentrates as the cheeses dry and age, so the amount of saturated fat isn't a great concern.

serves 4

---

4 large fresh figs, quartered

4 tablespoons extra virgin olive oil

1 tablespoon red-pepper flakes

1 pound fresh ricotta cheese
Sea salt to taste

1 tablespoon fig vincotto or aged balsamic vinegar

8 slices crusty bread, grilled or warmed in the oven

In a small bowl, toss the figs with the olive oil and pepper flakes. Using a spoon, smash the figs into a pastelike consistency.

Spoon the ricotta into the center of a large shallow bowl. Spoon the fig paste into the center. Sprinkle the sea salt on top and drizzle with the vincotto or balsamic vinegar. Serve family-style with the bread.

Radish, Apple, Hazelnut, and Arugula Salad

This is one of the all-time favorite salads at Little Beet, especially in those months when the ripe fresh vegetables of summer are just a memory. It's a study in contrasts and crunch. The apples and radish share the same crisp texture, but the apples are sweet while the radish counterpunches with sharpness. The arugula picks up on the sharp theme, while the hazelnuts bring sweet, buttery crunch into play. It is fascinating to me how varied and interesting a recipe can be with just a few ingredients. It just goes to show you that a small band can fill a room with music if the players are really good.

serves 4

1 tablespoon hazelnut oil

2 tablespoons canola oil

2 tablespoons white balsamic vinegar

1 tablespoon lemon juice

2 teaspoons honey

Salt and fresh ground black pepper to taste

1 pound baby arugula

2 medium Granny Smith apples, cored and thinly sliced

6 breakfast radishes, thinly sliced on a mandoline

2 tablespoons hazelnuts, toasted and coarsely chopped

In a medium bowl, whisk together the hazelnut oil, canola oil, vinegar, lemon juice, and honey. Season with salt and pepper.

In a salad bowl, combine the arugula, apples, radishes, and hazelnuts. Pour the vinaigrette over the arugula mixture and toss to coat. Season to taste with additional salt and pepper and serve.

SOUPS

Soups are meant to comfort the soul. At least that's the effect they have on me as I dip my spoon in, lean over the bowl, and get a whiff of delicious steam. Soups tend to marry flavors into one overall taste. Fats are particularly helpful in achieving this effect. They coat the palate to create a smooth feeling that extends flavor. They add body and richer mouth feel. Of course, I am not going to leave it at that if I have the opportunity to create an interesting contrast with some crunch by way of nuts or croutons.

Yellow Split Pea Soup | 26

Cauliflower-Leek Soup with Madras Curry and Almonds | 27

Acorn Squash Soup with Pistachios, | 28
Black Bread, and Apples

Butternut Squash Soup with Walnut Pesto | 31

Carrot and Ginger Soup | 32

Yellow Split Pea Soup

This is a somewhat multicultural soup. I cook down a classic French mirepoix (onion, celery, carrot, and garlic) in ghee, which is the Indian word for clarified butter. Yellow split peas are the main ingredient in dhal, the spiced pea soup of India. Closer to home, split peas are the universal soup of the day in the thousands of diners and roadside cafés where blue plate specials still rule. And while it may be universal, I often find the diner version unexciting. Adding curry powder, spicy cayenne, and dry white wine proves there is more one can do with split peas than throw them in a pot of water with ham hocks. I'll let you decide if you want to leave the end result rough and full bodied or if you would prefer to puree it. If you do puree, garnish with torn baby kale.

serves 4

1 tablespoon clarified butter

1 medium onion, cut into ½-inch dice

1 large rib celery, cut into ½-inch dice

1 large carrot, cut into ½-inch dice

2 cloves garlic, cut into ½-inch dice

1½ cups dried yellow split peas

2 teaspoons Madras curry powder

½ teaspoon cayenne pepper

¼ cup white wine

4 cups water or vegetable broth

Salt and fresh ground black pepper to taste

1 tablespoon chopped parsley

1 tablespoon chopped cilantro

Preheat a large heavy-bottomed pot over low heat for 5 minutes. Add the clarified butter, onion, celery, carrot, and garlic, cover, and sweat the vegetables until they are translucent, about 10 minutes.

Add the split peas, curry powder, and cayenne, and stir well to coat thoroughly with the mirepoix.

Add the white wine and cook until it has almost evaporated, using a wooden spoon to scrape up the bits on the bottom of the pan. Add the water or vegetable broth and simmer until a pea smashes easily when pressed against the side of the pot, 40 to 50 minutes. (The soup will have thickened.) Adjust the flavor with salt and pepper.

At this stage, if you prefer the soup to be smooth, puree it in a blender, in batches. If not, leave it chunky and thick. Garnish with the parsley and cilantro.

Cauliflower-Leek Soup with Madras Curry and Almonds

This humble and economical soup had a luxurious beginning. I originally presented it with butter-poached lobster floating in it. At some point I realized that the soup was special all on its own. Though vegetarian, it has the texture that you expect from the addition of loads of fat and cream. The secret? Cauliflower. When you process it in a blender, it is as velvety as the most unctuous cream sauce. Madras curry adds an exciting, flavorful pop. The Marcona almonds, which are from Spain, impart a crunch that makes each bite, slurp, or sip a little more interesting.

serves 4

---

1 large head cauliflower, coarsely chopped

2 medium leeks, white part only, chopped

3 cloves garlic

¼ cup clarified butter

1 teaspoon Madras curry powder

Juice of 1 lemon

Salt to taste

¼ cup Marcona almonds

1 teaspoon chopped parsley

In a large pot, combine the cauliflower, leeks, and garlic. Add water to cover, and bring to a simmer. Cook until the cauliflower falls apart, about 30 minutes. Do not drain.

Meanwhile, in a small saucepan over low heat, warm the clarified butter. Stir in the curry powder and cook for 5 minutes. Using a chinois, strain the butter and reserve both it and the curry powder.

Transfer the butter to the pot of cauliflower. Working in batches, puree the mixture in a blender. Season to taste with the lemon juice and salt. Add a little more water, if desired, to make a thinner soup.

In a medium bowl, combine the almonds and parsley. Add a pinch of the reserved curry powder and toss together. Season with lemon juice and salt to taste. Add a little more curry powder for a spicier soup.

Ladle the soup into bowls and garnish with the almond mixture. Serve hot.

Acorn Squash Soup with Pistachios, Black Bread, and Apples

Squash is such a good flavor absorber that I keep coming up with new things to do with it. With a little imagination and the ingredients in your fridge, you likely have the makings of a good squash soup. The combination here works as a complete meal, especially for, say, lunch on a cold winter weekend. The black bread croutons add crunch and body, and the apples call up hints of a savory apple crisp. For a heartier meal, skip blending the squash and serve it roasted, alongside duck breast or turkey leg. You can also substitute cauliflower for the acorn squash.

serves 4

1-2 pounds acorn squash, halved lengthwise

2 teaspoons butter

1 teaspoon light brown sugar

½ teaspoon ground cinnamon

Kosher salt and fresh ground black pepper to taste

2 quarts water

for the garnish:

1 teaspoon butter

1 large slice pumpernickel, cut into ¼-inch dice

1 medium Granny Smith apple, peeled, cored, and diced

2 tablespoons shelled pistachios

Salt and fresh ground black pepper to taste

Preheat the oven to 400°F for 15 minutes. Place the squash halves, cut side down, on a baking sheet. Do not remove the seeds. Bake until the skin is blistered and the flesh is fork-tender, about 35 to 40 minutes. Set aside to cool.

to make the garnish:

Meanwhile, in a medium saucepan over medium heat, melt the butter. Add the bread and cook, stirring frequently, until crispy, about 3 to 4 minutes. Transfer the bread to a medium bowl using a slotted spoon. Repeat with the apple, followed by the pistachios, sautéing until golden brown. Transfer to the bowl and toss together. Season with salt and pepper and set aside.

Scoop the flesh and seeds from the squash and transfer them to a large bowl. Add the butter, sugar, cinnamon, salt, pepper, and water. Working in batches, puree the mixture in a blender until smooth. Ladle into soup bowls and garnish with the bread mixture.

Butternut Squash Soup with Walnut Pesto

Everyone makes butternut squash soup, so how can we make it more interesting? The walnut pesto adds layers of flavor from herbs, funkiness from cheese, and crunch from the nuts—so the one-dimensional, everybody-makes-it standby is now a lot more interesting. I use Pecorino instead of Parmesan because it is sharper (I think of it as more "sheepy"), so it stands out instead of fading into the squash, which Parmesan will do.

serves 4

for the soup:

- 6 pounds butternut squash, halved lengthwise
- 1 quart water
- 3 tablespoons maple syrup
- 3 tablespoons honey
- 6 tablespoons butter
- 2 tablespoons salt
- 2 tablespoons ground cinnamon
- 1 tablespoon freshly grated nutmeg
- 1 tablespoon lemon juice
- 2 teaspoons fresh ground black pepper

for the pesto:

- ¼ cup walnuts, toasted and chopped
- 2 tablespoons grated Pecorino cheese
- 1 tablespoon walnut oil
- 1 tablespoon chopped parsley
- 1 teaspoon chopped sage
- Salt and fresh ground black pepper to taste

to make the soup:

Preheat the oven to 400°F. Place the squash (with seeds) cut side down in a roasting pan and fill with the water. Roast until the skin is completely blistered and the squash is fork-tender, about 45 minutes. Let cool.

to make the pesto:

Meanwhile, in a small bowl, combine the walnuts, cheese, walnut oil, parsley, sage, salt, and pepper. Set aside.

Scoop the flesh and seeds from the squash and transfer them to a large bowl. Add the maple syrup, honey, butter, salt, cinnamon, nutmeg, lemon juice, and pepper. Working in batches, puree the mixture in a blender until smooth. Ladle into soup bowls and garnish with the pesto.

Carrot and Ginger Soup

The tastes of sweet carrots and pungent ginger go together so well. In this simple soup, both ingredients are highlighted and really jump off the palate. I first made this combination as a sauce for a slow-cooked Moroccan spiced wild salmon dish that I serve with pickled beets. It was wildly popular, in part, I think, because of the vibrancy of the spiced carrot coating. So here you have the same elements—and big flavor—in the form of a soup. If you double the recipe, you can have soup for one meal, freeze the remaining amount, and use it as a sauce for salmon on one of those nights when you want something special but don't have the time to do much cooking. For added body, garnish with sautéed lobster, shrimp, or scallops and a sprinkling of chopped chives.

serves 4

½ cup butter or 6 tablespoons canola oil

1 pound carrots, peeled and thinly sliced

2 cloves garlic

1 tablespoon grated fresh ginger

½ teaspoon turmeric powder

¼ teaspoon cumin seeds, ground

Salt and fresh ground black pepper to taste

In a large pot over low heat, combine the butter or oil, carrots, garlic, ginger, turmeric, and cumin. Add water to cover, and cook until the carrots are tender, about 10 minutes. Working in batches, puree the mixture in a blender until smooth. Taste and adjust the flavor with salt and pepper. If desired, add water to thin the soup. Serve hot.

CHAPTER 3

MOSTLY GRAINS, MOSTLY GLUTEN-FREE

I think it's fair to say that most of humanity gets most of its nutrition from grains: wheat in the Western world, corn in the New World, rice in Asia, millet in Africa. I've also included quinoa in this section, which is not technically a grain; it sure tastes and acts like one and packs a good amount of protein. The grains and near grains in this section all share a toothsome texture and satisfy hunger pangs quite rapidly (probably because they are high in protein and carbohydrates). The problem is, left on their own, they are not that exciting in flavor. On the other side of the coin, though, they are unrivaled as flavor sponges and soak up dressings beautifully and, in so doing, become little flavor packets that punctuate every mouthful. Those of you who are gluten free, but still like grainy goodness, will be happy to find that all but one of these recipes (Farro Salad with Pickled Mushrooms, Golden Raisins, and Tender Greens) will fit into your diet.

Toasted Kasha with Mushrooms and Scallions   36

Quinoa, Beet, and Arugula Salad   37

Quinoa Tabbouleh with Feta Cheese and Cucumber   39

Black Quinoa with Pine Nuts, Scallions,   40
and Oranges, with Ginger Dressing

Toasted Almond Quinoa Pilaf   41

Quinoa, Feta Cheese, Raisins, and Pistachios   42

Barley with Onions and Pine Nuts   44

Barley Noodles in Mushroom and Onion Broth   45

Puffed Millet, Tomatoes, Jalapeño, and Avocado   47

Farro Salad with Pickled Mushrooms,   48
Golden Raisins, and Tender Greens

Wild Rice Salad with Kale, Pecans, and Oranges   50

Toasted Kasha with Mushrooms and Scallions

I loved my Grandma Rose's mushroom barley soup. And her kasha is right up there on my list of family favorites. Both were rib-sticking and hearty. Here I combine some of those flavors and textures and trade the heavy Eastern European interpretations for a dish that's bright and crunchy.

serves 4

for the stock:

1 tablespoon olive oil

4 cups mixed mushrooms (portobello, cremini, and oyster), stems removed and reserved for stock, bulbs sliced 1/4 inch thick

1 medium carrot, cut into small dice

1 medium onion, cut into small dice

1 large rib celery, cut into small dice

5 cups water

for the barley:

3 tablespoons olive oil

1 cup whole kasha

1 teaspoon grated lemon zest

6 sprigs fresh thyme, divided

2 tablespoons butter

1 small onion, cut into 1/4-inch dice

Salt and fresh ground black pepper to taste

4 tablespoons chopped scallions, green and white parts

3 tablespoons chopped parsley

2 tablespoons hazelnut oil

1 tablespoon hazelnuts, toasted and chopped

Juice of 1/2 lemon

to make the stock:

In a medium saucepan over medium-high heat, warm the olive oil until it begins to ripple. Add the mushroom stems and cook until they have released their liquid and begin to brown. Add the carrot, onion, and celery and cook until browned. Add the water, bring to a boil, and cook until reduced by half, about 10 minutes. Strain and set aside.

to make the barley:

In a medium saucepan over medium heat, warm the olive oil until it begins to ripple. Add the kasha and cook, stirring constantly, until it is fragrant, about 5 minutes. Add the lemon zest, 3 sprigs of the thyme, and 2 1/4 cups of the reserved mushroom stock. Bring to a simmer, cover, and reduce the heat to low. Cook, stirring occasionally, until the kasha is firm but collapses under the pressure of your fingers when pressing it together, 25 to 30 minutes. Transfer to a strainer and remove and discard the thyme. Immediately rinse the kasha under cool running water to remove any of the starchiness.

In a medium saucepan over low heat, melt the butter. Add the onion and cook, stirring frequently, until tender and translucent, about 5 minutes. Add the mushroom slices and the remaining 3 sprigs thyme and continue to cook until the mushrooms are brown, 8 to 10 minutes. Remove and discard the thyme.

In a serving bowl, combine the kasha and mushroom mixture and toss. Season to taste with salt and pepper. Set aside to cool.

Meanwhile, in a small bowl, whisk together the scallions, parsley, hazelnut oil, hazelnuts, lemon juice, and salt and pepper to taste. Pour over the buckwheat mixture and toss to coat. Season to taste with additional salt and pepper before serving.

Quinoa, Beet, and Arugula Salad

Quinoa is a seed, though it looks like a grain and, when it comes to cooking, acts like a grain. You can use it as a gluten-free replacement for barley, couscous, or millet, or farro. Actually, its closest relative—according to botanists—is the beet, and like beets, it is highly alkaline—which is the opposite of sour. That means that it always works well with tangy acidic dressings. In this case, I dress it with lemon juice and top it with beets marinated in honey, vinegar, and Dijon mustard.

serves 4

for the quinoa:

- 2 tablespoons canola oil
- ½ medium onion, cut into ¼-inch dice
- 1½ cups quinoa, rinsed under cold running water for 10 minutes
- 3 cups water
- 1 clove garlic
- 1 bay leaf
- 1 sprig thyme
- 2 teaspoons salt
- 2 tablespoons extra virgin olive oil
- Zest and juice of 1 lemon

for the beets:

- ½ pound baby golden beets
- 3 tablespoons olive oil, divided
- Salt and fresh ground black pepper to taste
- ½ pound baby red beets
- 1 tablespoon sherry vinegar
- 1 tablespoon honey
- 1 teaspoon Dijon mustard
- ¼ pound baby candy striped beets, sliced on a mandoline
- 4 ounces baby arugula

to make the quinoa:

Preheat a 2-quart pot over low heat for 3 minutes. Add the canola oil and the onion and sweat until the onion is soft and translucent, about 3 minutes. Add the quinoa and stir to coat with the oil. Add the water, increase the heat, and bring to a boil. Add the garlic, bay leaf, and thyme. Cover and simmer until the germ opens and it inflates in size, 25 to 30 minutes. Add the salt, olive oil, lemon zest, and lemon juice. Fluff with a fork. Remove from the heat and let sit, covered, for 10 minutes. Remove and discard the thyme, garlic, and bay leaf.

to make the beets:

Preheat the oven to 350°F. In a small bowl, toss the golden beets in 1 tablespoon of the olive oil. Season with salt and pepper and wrap in foil. Repeat with the baby red beets. Roast until fork-tender, about 30 minutes. Peel the beets while still hot under cool running water. Quarter the golden beets and transfer to a medium bowl. Quarter the red beets and transfer to a second bowl.

In a small bowl, whisk together the remaining 1 tablespoon olive oil, vinegar, honey, and mustard. Divide between the beets and toss to coat. Cover and marinate for 1 hour in the refrigerator.

In a serving bowl, combine the quinoa, golden and red beets, candy striped beets, and arugula and toss. Season with salt and pepper before serving.

Quinoa Tabbouleh with Feta Cheese and Cucumber

Quinoa is a great non-gluten substitute for the bulgur wheat that is called for in traditional tabbouleh recipes. If you are not in a hurry, let the quinoa cool overnight. It gets nice and fluffy, which strikes just the right note of contrast to the crisp summery crunch and tang of the other ingredients. Dress it at the last moment so it doesn't get soggy. On many summer evenings, especially the super-hot ones, I make this salad and call it dinner.

serves 4

for the quinoa:

- 2 tablespoons canola oil
- ½ onion, diced
- 1½ cups quinoa, rinsed under cold running water for 10 minutes
- 3 cups water
- 1 clove garlic
- 1 bay leaf
- 1 sprig thyme
- 2 teaspoons salt
- 2 tablespoons extra virgin olive oil
- Zest and juice of 1 lemon

for the salad:

- ½ cup diced feta cheese
- ½ cup diced cucumber
- ½ cup diced tomatoes
- 3 tablespoons chopped fresh parsley
- 1 tablespoon chopped fresh dill
- 1 teaspoon lemon zest
- Salt and fresh ground black pepper to taste

to make the quinoa:

In a medium pot over low heat, combine the canola oil and onion. Sweat the onion until soft and translucent, about 3 minutes. Add the quinoa and stir to coat with the oil. Add the water, increase the heat, and bring to a boil. Add the garlic, bay leaf, and thyme. Cover and simmer until the germ opens and it inflates in size, 25 to 30 minutes. Add the salt, olive oil, lemon zest, and lemon juice. Fluff with a fork. Remove from the heat and let sit, covered, for 10 minutes. Remove and discard the garlic, bay leaf, and thyme.

to make the salad:

Spread the quinoa on a rimmed baking sheet to cool. Once cool, transfer to a serving bowl. Add the feta, cucumber, tomatoes, parsley, dill, and lemon zest. Season with salt and pepper. Serve chilled or at room temperature.

Black Quinoa with Pine Nuts, Scallions, and Oranges, with Ginger Dressing

Black quinoa is one of those lucky accidents that Mother Nature occasionally arranges for us. In the mid-1980s, two Colorado farmers who had planted quinoa were surprised to harvest a black crop, rather than the red or brown they expected. It turned out that their quinoa had crossbred with a wild relative, Lamb's Quarter, and the offspring was an earthier, crunchier quinoa. Like its tamer cousin, black quinoa is higher in heart-healthy fatty acids than wheat. I like the way the look of a black background makes vegetables pop with vibrant color, especially in the gray days of winter. It's also a great backdrop for fruit.

serves 4

for the quinoa:

- 2 tablespoons canola oil
- ½ onion, diced
- 1½ cups black quinoa, rinsed under cold running water for 10 minutes
- 3 cups water
- 1 clove garlic
- 1 bay leaf
- 1 sprig thyme
- 2 teaspoons salt
- 2 tablespoons extra virgin olive oil
- Zest and juice of 1 lemon
- ½ cup toasted pine nuts
- 3 scallions, thinly sliced
- 3 oranges, sectioned, seeds and pith removed

for the dressing:

- 4 tablespoons extra virgin olive oil
- 2 tablespoons ginger juice (page 16)
- 2 tablespoons lemon juice
- 1 tablespoon apple cider vinegar
- Salt and fresh ground black pepper to taste

to make the quinoa:

In a small pot over low heat, combine the canola oil and onion. Sweat the onion until soft and translucent, about 3 minutes. Add the quinoa and stir to coat with the oil. Add the water, increase the heat, and bring to a boil. Add the garlic, bay leaf, and thyme. Cover and simmer until the germ opens and it inflates in size, 25 to 30 minutes. Add the salt, olive oil, lemon zest, and lemon juice. Fluff with a fork. Remove from the heat and let sit, covered, for 10 minutes. Remove and discard the garlic, bay leaf, and thyme.

to make the dressing:

In a small bowl, whisk together the olive oil, ginger juice, lemon juice, and vinegar. Season to taste with salt and pepper. Pour over the quinoa and toss to coat. Set aside to cool. Taste and adjust the seasonings. Transfer to a serving platter and garnish with the pine nuts, scallions, and oranges.

Toasted Almond Quinoa Pilaf

Pilaf, the Turkish preparation of rice in seasoned broth, herbs, and catch-as-catch-can ingredients, was very popular when I started my restaurant in the '80s. It was a way to make rice more interesting. Turns out the same approach makes all grains (and grainlike foods such as quinoa) more fun. Then there is the fabulous Marcona almond, which is smaller and sweeter than your average California almond. They're blanched and then roasted in olive oil. Yes, you could use regular roasted almonds, but what a difference!

serves 4

2 tablespoons canola oil

½ medium onion, diced

1½ cups quinoa, rinsed under cold running water for 10 minutes

3 cups water

1 clove garlic

1 bay leaf

1 sprig thyme

2 teaspoons salt

2 tablespoons extra virgin olive oil

Zest and juice of 1 lemon

Salt and fresh ground black pepper to taste

½ cup Marcona almonds, toasted

1 tablespoon fresh parsley leaves

1 tablespoon fresh mint leaves

1 teaspoon lemon zest

In a small pot over low heat, combine the canola oil and onion. Sweat the onion until soft and translucent, about 3 minutes. Add the quinoa and stir to coat with the oil. Add the water, increase the heat, and bring to a boil. Add the garlic, bay leaf, and thyme. Cover and simmer until the germ opens and it inflates in size, 25 to 30 minutes. Add the salt, olive oil, lemon zest, and lemon juice. Fluff with a fork. Remove from the heat and let sit, covered, for 10 minutes. Remove and discard the garlic, bay leaf, and thyme.

Spread the quinoa on a rimmed baking sheet to cool. Once cool, transfer to a serving bowl. Season with salt and pepper. Toss with the almonds, parsley, mint, and lemon zest. Serve at room temperature or chilled.

Quinoa, Feta Cheese, Raisins, and Pistachios

For this dish, quinoa takes on a Greek profile with the flavors of oregano, mint, and parsley. I often add plumped raisins and pistachios to salads the way other people think of salt and pepper with a fried egg. It's rarely wrong. In fact, it never is. Add raisins and pistachios to any salad—even if it doesn't call for them; there's no reason not to give them a shot. And let me know how it turns out!

serves 4

2 tablespoons canola oil

½ onion, diced

1½ cups quinoa, rinsed under cold running water for 10 minutes

3 cups water

1 clove garlic

1 bay leaf

1 sprig thyme

2 teaspoons salt

2 tablespoons + ½ cup extra virgin olive oil

Zest and juice of 1 lemon

Salt and fresh ground black pepper to taste

½ cup diced feta cheese

¼ cup raisins, plumped in warm water

¼ cup toasted pistachios

1 tablespoon parsley leaves

1 tablespoon oregano leaves

1 tablespoon mint leaves

¼ cup red wine vinegar

In a small pot over low heat, combine the canola oil and onion. Sweat the onion until soft and translucent, about 3 minutes. Add the quinoa and stir to coat with the oil. Add the water, increase the heat, and bring to a boil. Add the garlic, bay leaf, and thyme. Cover and simmer until the germ opens and it inflates in size, 25 to 30 minutes. Add the salt, 2 tablespoons of the olive oil, lemon zest, and lemon juice. Fluff with a fork. Remove from the heat and let sit, covered, for 10 minutes. Remove and discard the garlic, bay leaf, and thyme.

Spread the quinoa on a rimmed baking sheet to cool. Once cool, season with salt and pepper, then transfer to a serving bowl. Add the feta, raisins, pistachios, parsley, oregano, and mint.

In a small bowl, whisk together the remaining ½ cup olive oil, vinegar, and salt and pepper to taste. Pour over the quinoa mixture and toss to coat. Serve at room temperature or chilled.

Barley with Onions and Pine Nuts

Barley is a great source of eight essential amino acids, and like many whole grains, it will not spike blood sugar levels the way that more refined grains will. Cooking the barley by first sweating it with onion and carrot helps lock in flavor from the very beginning. The herbs and nuts transform this stick-to-your-ribs peasant dish into a light salad that I often serve with fish or roast chicken. It's also my go-to side with wild salmon.

serves 4

2 tablespoons canola oil

¾ cup finely chopped onion

1 tablespoon minced garlic

½ cup diced carrot

1 pound pearled barley, rinsed and soaked overnight in water

4 thyme sprigs

1 bay leaf

1½ tablespoons parsley leaves

Zest and juice of ½ lemon

Salt and fresh ground black pepper to taste

6 tablespoons pine nuts, toasted

In a small pot over low heat, combine the canola oil and onion. Sweat until the onion is translucent, about 5 minutes. Add the garlic and carrot and sweat for 5 minutes. Add the barley and stir to coat evenly with the oil. Add enough boiling water to cover. Add the thyme and bay leaf, increase the heat to high, and return to a boil. Reduce the heat and simmer, covered, for 15 minutes. Remove from the heat and remove and discard the thyme and bay leaf.

Add the parsley, lemon zest, and lemon juice. Season with salt and pepper. Toss gently and garnish with the pine nuts.

Barley Noodles in Mushroom and Onion Broth

One of the secrets of New York dining is how well you can eat for not very much money in Korea Town on 32nd Street. This recipe is inspired by the barley noodles, tofu, and some seasonings from my dining experiences in Korea Town. I also borrowed from Japanese influences: kombu, rice wine vinegar, tamari, and shochu, which is distilled from barley, sweet potatoes, buckwheat, and rice. The pine nuts and oyster mushrooms are a study in contrasting textures. The result? A delicious melting pot comprised of a melding of food cultures.

serves 4

8 ounces dry barley noodles

2 tablespoons canola oil

4 ounces shiitake mushrooms, stems trimmed, cut in half

4 ounces oyster mushrooms, stems trimmed, cut in half

2 small onions, thinly sliced in half-moons

1 teaspoon sugar

3 cloves garlic, thinly sliced

1 teaspoon Korean red chili powder

3 tablespoons shochu or sake

1 tablespoon rice wine vinegar

1 ounce dry kombu, wiped clean with a damp cloth

1 tablespoon tamari sauce

Sea salt to taste

2 ounces firm tofu, diced

1 teaspoon sesame oil

1/4 cup pine nuts, toasted

Prepare the barley noodles according to package directions and set aside. Meanwhile, in a 2-quart saucepan over medium heat, warm the canola oil. Add the shiitake and oyster mushrooms and cook until they release their liquid and begin to brown. Add the onions and cook until they begin to caramelize. Stir in the sugar, garlic, and chili powder and cook for 5 minutes. Add the shochu or sake and the vinegar and, using a wooden spoon, scrape up the browned bits on the bottom of the pan.

Add the kombu. Add enough water to just cover, bring to a simmer, and continue to simmer for 30 minutes. Using tongs, remove the kombu and slice into thin strips. Add the tamari and sea salt and taste and adjust the seasonings. Add the cooked noodles. Ladle into bowls and garnish with the tofu, a drizzle of sesame oil, and some pine nuts.

Puffed Millet, Tomatoes, Jalapeño, and Avocado

My search for gluten-free grains brought me to this African staple that Nigerians traditionally make into a porridge but is also available in airy, slightly chewy, ready-to-use cereal known as puffed millet. I soon discovered that there are many flavorful possibilities for this mild-mannered grain. It easily takes on the taste and aroma of other ingredients. I first started to play with it in the summertime; hence the diced tomatoes. The truly scintillating dressing of jalapeño, lime, and cilantro works its magic here.

serves 4

1 cup diced tomatoes

1 avocado, diced

1 jalapeño chile pepper, seeded and minced (wear plastic gloves when handling)

3 tablespoons fresh lime juice

2 tablespoons extra virgin olive oil

1 tablespoon chopped cilantro

Salt and fresh ground black pepper to taste

1 cup puffed millet

In a large bowl, combine the tomatoes, avocado, jalapeño pepper, lime juice, olive oil, cilantro, and salt and black pepper. Add the millet and toss to coat. Serve chilled or at room temperature.

Farro Salad with Pickled Mushrooms, Golden Raisins, and Tender Greens

Dressed with nothing but lemon and olive oil, sweet, nutty farro and tangy pickled mushrooms get together in this toothsome salad. Farro is an ancient relative of wheat, yet it has far less gluten. It has lots of grain nutrients, as do most whole, unprocessed grains. Texturally, it has the fullness of barley. I first tasted farro at Gramercy Tavern when Tom Colicchio was the chef there in 1994. He used stone-ground whole farro grains, which retain more bran and fiber so they don't convert to sugar so rapidly.

serves 4

for the pickled mushrooms:

- ½ cup white balsamic vinegar
- ½ cup water
- 1 tablespoon pickling spice
- 1 tablespoon red-pepper flakes
- 1 tablespoon kosher salt
- 1 cup mixed mushrooms, such as button, cremini, and oyster

for the farro:

- 4 quarts water
- 1 tablespoon salt
- 1 cup whole farro
- ¼ cup golden raisins
- ¼ cup olive oil
  Juice of 2 small lemons
- 1 tablespoon fresh parsley leaves
- ½ cup greens such as arugula, red oak, or tatsoi, or a mixture
  Salt and fresh ground black pepper to taste

to make the pickled mushrooms:

In a medium pot, combine the vinegar, water, the pickling spice, pepper flakes, and salt and bring to a boil. Remove from the heat. Plunge the mushrooms into the liquid and set aside to cool, uncovered. Place in the refrigerator overnight or longer, depending on how strong you want the pickled mushrooms.

to make the farro:

In a large pot, bring the water to a boil. Add the salt and return to a boil. Add the farro and cook until firm and toothsome but not hard, about 20 minutes. Remove from the heat and let stand for 2 minutes.

Drain the farro and transfer to a large bowl. Add the raisins, olive oil, lemon juice, and parsley. Toss to thoroughly combine. Set aside to cool.

With a slotted spoon, remove the mushrooms from the liquid and add to the farro. Add the greens. Toss, season with salt and black pepper, and serve at room temperature.

Wild Rice Salad with Kale, Pecans, and Oranges

Wild rice isn't really rice. Maybe you knew that already, but I was well into my career before I learned that it is a grass that is harvested by Native Americans, especially along the shores of Minnesota's many lakes. When I put together the menu for Little Beet, I was always looking to do things with gluten-free grains. Instead of mixing wild rice with brown rice or vermicelli, which are common combinations, I decided to let it star on its own along with another New World surprise, pecans. I say surprise because in the same way that wild rice isn't rice, scientists tell us that pecans are not true nuts. Botanically speaking, they are fruits (the technical word is *drupe*), and they taste nutty and buttery no matter what the textbooks say. With the flavor of oranges as a top note and the grassiness of kale in the background, this salad tastes especially bright and full-flavored and is also pretty. Nutrition bonus: Wild rice has a higher protein content than "real" rice, millet, or barley.

serves 4

4 peppercorns

1 clove garlic

1 bay leaf

1 sprig thyme

1 cup wild rice, rinsed

2 cups water

1 bunch kale, tough stems removed, chopped coarsely

1 cup pecan halves, toasted

2 medium oranges, segmented, juice reserved

6 tablespoons extra virgin olive oil

Juice of 1 lemon

1 tablespoon white balsamic vinegar

1 tablespoon honey

Salt and fresh ground black pepper to taste

Wrap the peppercorns, garlic, bay leaf, and thyme in cheesecloth and secure with kitchen string. In a medium saucepan, combine the wild rice with the water and the herb packet. Bring to a simmer over low heat. Simmer, covered, until the wild rice is tender, about 50 minutes. Let cool for 30 minutes. Remove and discard the herb packet.

Transfer the wild rice to a serving bowl. Add the kale, pecans, and orange segments and toss to combine.

In a small bowl, combine the reserved orange juice, olive oil, lemon juice, balsamic vinegar, honey, and salt and black pepper. Add to the wild rice mixture. Season to taste with additional salt and black pepper and serve chilled or at room temperature.

CHAPTER 4

SEAFOOD

As far as healthy fats go, seafood hits the bull's-eye: If you are looking for food with a healthy fat profile, any seafood at all fits that description. Then, as an added benefit, oily fish such as salmon, trout, mackerel, anchovies, and bluefish—to name a few—are quite high in omega-3s, which are super protective of heart health. The texture of seafood is satisfyingly meaty, no doubt because seafood is rich in protein. The flavor is, in most cases, quite mild, which means that you can match it with so many different ingredients. And stronger-flavored fish (like the aforementioned oil-rich creatures) can stand up to powerful spices, seasonings, marinades, and dressings without fading into the background.

Ceviche of Snapper with Avocado and Cilantro | 57

Gambas al Ajillo (Shrimp with Garlic and Oil) | 58

Grilled Shrimp Arrabbiata with Chickpeas
and Broccoli | 59

Grilled Shrimp with Black Quinoa,
Avocado, and Oranges | 60

Coconut- and Macadamia-Dusted Shrimp
with Tropical Fruit Salad | 63

Shrimp Semi-Ceviche Cara Cara | 65

Clams Steamed in Sake with Soy and Pine Nuts | 67

Stewed Clams and Mussels with Garlic
and Vinho Verde | 68

Squid Confit with White Bean Stifado | 69

Seafood Boudin | 70

Rock Lobster Tails with Garlic and Oil | 73

Grilled Octopus Greek Style | 74

Salmon, Grapefruit, Olive Oil, and Arugula | 76

Grilled Salmon, Lentils, Avocado, and Pecans, 77
with Sherry Vinaigrette

The Five Fat Challenge: Salmon-Avocado Caponata 79
with Pistachios and Black Olive Oil

TokyoVietnam Tuna Wrap 80

Grilled Spanish Mackerel with Black Olives, 81
Tomatoes, and Pistou

Tuna Cubes with Citrus Soy, Chives, and Cucumber 82

Mackerel, Oranges, Mint, Chiles, and Lemon Agrumato 85

Olive Oil–Poached Cod with Roasted Tomato 86
and Peppers

Grilled Sea Bass with Spigarello, Chiles, and Garlic 89

Grilled Sea Bream with Lemon Gremolata and Spinach 90

Grilled Striped Bass with Sweet Peppers, 93
New Potatoes, and Pesto

Broiled Local Flounder Oreganata with Charred Broccoli 94

Ceviche of Snapper with Avocado and Cilantro

Ceviche is a form of "non-cooking cooking." I know that sounds wrong, but what I mean is that in making ceviche, instead of using heat to break down the proteins, we use acid—citrus juice—to break down protein. The fruits also lend beautiful flavor, and honey rounds it out even more. I am told that this form of "cooking" originated with Native American fishermen who wanted to prepare their catch while at sea, but didn't or couldn't build a fire. Makes sense. I wouldn't want a fire in my canoe or kayak. Make sure the fish is ice cold and the avocado is room temperature for a great experience.

serves 4

Juice of 1 medium orange

¼ cup lemon juice

¼ cup lime juice

1 pound sushi-grade fresh snapper fillet, thinly sliced

Sea salt to taste

1 tablespoon whole cilantro leaves

2 medium avocados, halved

1 medium orange, sectioned, membrane and pith removed

1 small serrano chile pepper, seeded and minced (wear plastic gloves when handling)

1 tablespoon acacia honey

In a shallow dish, combine the orange juice, lemon juice, and lime juice. Add the snapper, cover, and marinate in the refrigerator for 1 hour.

Remove the fish from the marinade and season it to taste with sea salt and cilantro. If desired, add some more lemon or lime juice to taste.

Place an avocado half on each of 4 plates. Top with the seasoned fish and arrange the orange segments around it. Sprinkle the chile pepper over the fish and season with additional sea salt. Drizzle with honey before serving.

Gambas al Ajillo (Shrimp with Garlic and Oil)

Ask anyone who has ever visited Madrid to name their favorite meals and my bet is the list will include the wonderful little shrimp in hot olive oil and garlic from the famous hole-in-the-wall restaurant in the Old Town named Casa del Abuelo. There is something bordering on alchemy from the combination of shrimp, garlic, and oil. It is nutty, sweet, and . . . well . . . shrimpy. I throw in a little lemon zest to brighten things up. This recipe is most often made with tiny shrimp, but fresh ones are hard to find in the United States. Don't waste your money on the frozen ones; deep-fried paper towels will probably taste as good. Medium shrimp are fine. So are large ones. Be sure to serve with crusty bread to mop up the garlicky oil. Spanish pimenton is available in powdered and whole form; I use the whole version here, also known as piri piri.

serves 4

---

25 fresh medium shrimp, peeled and deveined

Sea salt and fresh ground black pepper to taste

¼ cup extra virgin olive oil

6 cloves garlic, thinly sliced on a mandoline

1 hot Spanish pimenton, diced

¼ cup white wine

¼ cup lemon juice

1 tablespoon lemon zest

1 tablespoon chopped parsley

Season the shrimp with sea salt and pepper and set aside. In a heavy-bottomed frying pan or cast-iron skillet over medium heat, warm the olive oil and garlic until the garlic begins to brown slightly.

Add the pimenton, wine, lemon juice, and lemon zest and cook until the flavors begin to meld together, about 3 minutes. Increase the heat to high, slip the shrimp into the pan, and cook until the shrimp turn opaque throughout, 3 to 4 minutes. Taste and adjust the sea salt and pepper, garnish with the parsley, and serve with crusty bread.

Grilled Shrimp Arrabbiata with Chickpeas and Broccoli

This spicy Italian sauce, usually served over pasta, has been a lifelong favorite. But why, I wondered, does it always need pasta? Turns out it doesn't, so I took away the pasta and added broccoli, and shrimp for a more balanced meal. In Puglia, pasta is often paired with chickpeas, so I decided to substitute these healthy legumes for a pasta-free version. Make sure the broccoli is cooked to a soft but not mushy texture rather than a hard and crunchy one.

serves 4

for the shrimp:

- 2 tablespoons olive oil
- Juice of 1 medium lemon
- 3 cloves garlic
- 5 sprigs thyme
- Salt and fresh ground black pepper to taste
- 16 jumbo shrimp, peeled and deveined

for the chickpeas:

- 4 tablespoons olive oil
- 1 tablespoon red-pepper flakes
- 5 cloves garlic, thinly sliced
- 2 cups chopped fresh plum tomatoes
- 1 cup canned chickpeas, rinsed and drained
- 1 pound broccoli, tough stem ends removed and cut into 2-inch pieces
- 1 tablespoon chopped parsley
- Salt and fresh ground black pepper to taste

to make the shrimp:

In a shallow dish, combine the olive oil, lemon juice, garlic, thyme, and salt and black pepper. Add the shrimp and set aside to marinate for 30 minutes.

Preheat a grill pan over high heat for 5 minutes. Working in batches, grill the shrimp until opaque, about 1½ minutes per side. Transfer to a plate.

to make the chickpeas:

In a medium saucepan over medium-high heat, warm the olive oil until it ripples. Add the pepper flakes and cook for 30 seconds, or until fragrant. Add the garlic and tomatoes, reduce the heat, and simmer, uncovered, for 15 minutes. Stir in the chickpeas and cook for 5 minutes. Add the broccoli and cook until tender but not mushy, about 5 minutes.

Transfer the ragout to a serving bowl, top with the shrimp, and garnish with the parsley. Season with salt and black pepper.

Grilled Shrimp with Black Quinoa, Avocado, and Oranges

There are few salads that I make that offer the variety of taste and texture that this one does. I often have it for a winter lunch; it's perfect for getting through the day when you are looking at a heavier, heartier dinner. Don't be shy with the red-pepper flakes. They really wake up your tastebuds.

serves 4

for the shrimp:

- 2 tablespoons extra virgin olive oil
- 2 cloves garlic
- 2 sprigs thyme
- 1 teaspoon red-pepper flakes
- Salt and fresh ground black pepper to taste
- 12 jumbo shrimp, peeled and deveined

for the quinoa:

- 2 tablespoons canola oil
- 1/2 onion, diced
- 1 1/2 cups black quinoa, rinsed under cold running water for 10 minutes
- 3 cups water
- 1 clove garlic
- 1 bay leaf
- 1 sprig thyme
- 2 teaspoons salt
- 2 tablespoons extra virgin olive oil
- 1 tablespoon lemon zest
- 1/4 cup lemon juice

for the salad:

- 1 medium avocado
- 1 tablespoon extra virgin olive oil
- 1 Cara Cara or navel orange, segmented, juices reserved
- Juice of 1 medium lemon
- Salt and fresh ground black pepper to taste
- 1 tablespoon whole mint leaves
- 1 tablespoon whole parsley leaves
- 1/4 teaspoon red-pepper flakes

to make the shrimp:

In a shallow dish, combine the olive oil, garlic, thyme, pepper flakes, and salt and black pepper. Add the shrimp and toss to coat. Set aside while cooking the quinoa.

to make the quinoa:

In a saucepan over low heat, combine the canola oil and onion. Sweat the onion until soft and translucent, about 3 minutes. Add the quinoa and stir. Add the water, increase the heat, and bring to a boil. Add the garlic, bay leaf, and thyme. Cover and simmer until the germ opens and it inflates in size, 25 to 30 minutes. Add the salt, olive oil, lemon zest, and lemon juice. Fluff with a fork. Remove from the heat and let sit, covered, for 10 minutes. Remove and discard the bay leaf and thyme.

Preheat a cast-iron grill pan over high heat for 5 minutes. Working in batches, grill the shrimp until they turn opaque throughout, about 1 1/2 minutes per side. Transfer to a plate.

to assemble the salad:

Halve the avocado, remove the pit, and cut into medium dice. Transfer to a serving bowl. In a small bowl, combine the olive oil, reserved orange juice, orange segments, lemon juice, and salt and black pepper. Pour over the avocado. Add the warm quinoa and gently toss. Add the mint, parsley, and pepper flakes and top with the shrimp. Season with additional salt and black pepper to taste.

Coconut- and Macadamia- Dusted Shrimp with Tropical Fruit Salad

There was a time when it seemed any bar you walked into served coconut-crusted shrimp, deep fried and dripping with fatty calories. People love everything about them . . . except for the dripping with calories part. Mine are made with one part dried coconut and two parts macadamia nuts, which have healthier fat. Rather than frying, I "toast" the ingredients by sautéing them in just a little oil. You get all the crunch with far fewer fatty calories. As for the salad, it includes just about all of my favorite flavors and textures, many of them Asian.

serves 4

for the shrimp:

16 large shrimp, peeled, deveined, and halved lengthwise

Salt and fresh ground black pepper to taste

2 tablespoons canola oil

for the crumble:

⅓ cup roasted, salted macadamia nuts, coarsely chopped

2 tablespoons dried unsweetened coconut flakes

2 tablespoons panko bread crumbs, toasted in a skillet on low heat for 5 minutes

1 tablespoon lime zest

¼ cup lime juice

1 tablespoon soy sauce

1 tablespoon finely chopped scallions

Salt and fresh ground black pepper to taste

for the tropical fruit salad:

1 medium mango, cut into matchsticks

1 small pineapple, cut into matchsticks

1 medium green mango, cut into matchsticks

2 ounces jicama, cut into matchsticks

½ small daikon radish, cut into matchsticks

2 scallions, cut into matchsticks

2 tablespoons canola oil

2 tablespoons fresh lime juice

1 tablespoon rice wine vinegar

1 tablespoon Thai fish sauce

1 tablespoon cilantro leaves

1 tablespoon grated fresh ginger

1 teaspoon minced Thai red chile pepper (wear plastic gloves when handling)

Salt to taste

(continued on page 64)

to make the shrimp:

Season the shrimp with salt and pepper. In a large skillet over medium-high heat, warm the canola oil until it ripples. Working in batches, sauté the shrimp until they are opaque, about 1½ to 2 minutes per side. With a slotted spoon, transfer to a large shallow dish.

to make the crumble:

In a small bowl, combine the macadamia nuts, coconut, and panko. Scatter over the shrimp. Toss to thoroughly coat each one. Add the lime zest, lime juice, soy sauce, and scallions and toss. Season with salt and pepper.

to make the salad:

In a large bowl, combine the mango, pineapple, green mango, jicama, radish, scallions, canola oil, lime juice, vinegar, fish sauce, cilantro, ginger, and red chile pepper. Toss and season to taste with salt. Divide the salad among 4 plates and top each serving with 4 shrimp.

Shrimp Semi-Ceviche Cara Cara

Shellfish, shrimp, squid, and octopus often have sweeter flesh than true fin fish. They are a very good match for Cara Cara oranges—a cousin of navel oranges—which have just enough acid to cook the tender flesh while adding a little sweetness. One of my tricks is to blanch the seafood. This keeps it tender and succulent. The classic ceviche method, which doesn't involve blanching, uses acid only. This will make the flesh firmer. But who wants a firm scallop, tough shrimp, or rubbery squid? You can make this well in advance, something you wouldn't try with a regular fish ceviche because it will "overcook."

serves 4

5 ounces fresh lemon juice, divided

1 tablespoon honey

1 teaspoon + 1 tablespoon sea salt

1 quart water

6 ounces squid, cleaned and cut into rings

8 medium shrimp, peeled and deveined, cut in half lengthwise

6 ounces scallops, sliced width-wise

2 small jalapeño chile peppers, seeded and diced (wear plastic gloves when handling)

2 large Cara Cara oranges, sectioned, juice reserved

1 medium fennel bulb, trimmed, cored, and thinly sliced on a mandoline

½ cup whole mint leaves

1 tablespoon olive oil

In a stainless steel pot, combine half the lemon juice, the honey, and 1 teaspoon of the sea salt with the water and bring to a boil. Turn off the heat and add the squid. Poach for 1 minute, then remove to a serving bowl. With the pot off the heat, repeat with the shrimp and scallops, poaching each for 1 minute and transferring to the serving bowl.

Add the jalapeño peppers, remaining lemon juice, and orange juice to the bowl. Set aside to marinate for 5 minutes. Add the fennel, orange segments, mint, and remaining 1 tablespoon sea salt and toss. Drizzle the olive oil over and serve.

Clams Steamed in Sake with Soy and Pine Nuts

In recent years, you may have read about *umami,* the mysterious fifth taste. If you're still having a hard time recognizing it, though, I'm going to take you right to the source. The Japanese were the first to identify this taste in dashi—the broth that is so central to their cuisine. It is made with kombu (a form of seaweed or kelp), dried bonito flakes, and water. I spike mine with sake, and the rest of the recipe carries home the Asian theme with tofu and tamari. The finished dish is a mix of tastes and textures that I think of as Japanese clams casino. When you eat it, remember that in Japanese, *umami* means "deliciousness."

serves 4

½ cup dry sake

1 ounce kombu, rinsed

2 cups water

2 dozen littleneck clams, washed

6 ounces firm tofu, cut into ¼-inch pieces

¼ cup tamari soy sauce

3½ tablespoons pine nuts, toasted

2 scallions, thinly sliced

In a large pot, combine the sake, kombu, and water and bring to a simmer. Remove the kombu and reserve. Add the clams to the pot, cover, and simmer until the clams open. Add the tofu, soy sauce, pine nuts, and scallions to the pot. Slice the kombu into thin strips and add it back to the pot. Simmer until the tofu is heated through. Ladle the clams with their broth into shallow bowls and serve hot.

Stewed Clams and Mussels with Garlic and Vinho Verde

Portuguese food is not very well known in the United States (unless you have the good fortune to find yourself in a restaurant in Massachusetts or Rhode Island, where many Portuguese settled in the last century). A few years ago, I made my first trip to the sun-washed seaside city of Cascais, Portugal. When I tasted the simply prepared shellfish served everywhere, my reaction was, "Where have you been all my life?" I was particularly taken with a bowl of freshly caught shellfish steamed in white wine and sea water. Couldn't have been simpler, couldn't have been better. Of course, we washed it down with vinho verde, the famous fresh and fruity wine that has quenched many a Portuguese thirst. Here is my homage to that meal, the wine, and a beautiful city by the sea.

You might wonder why I use chicken stock instead of clam juice. I find it gives a meatier overall flavor; you get plenty of clam and mussel juice from the shellfish as they steam open.

serves 4

¼ cup extra virgin olive oil, plus more for drizzling

1 pound Manila clams

1 pound Bouchot or Prince Edward Island mussels, scrubbed and debearded

½ teaspoon red-pepper flakes

4 cloves garlic, sliced

¼ cup vinho verde

¼ cup chicken stock

Salt and fresh ground black pepper to taste

2 tablespoons parsley, cut into thin ribbons

Zest and juice of 1 lemon

Crusty Italian bread

In a large pot over medium-high heat, warm the olive oil. Add the clams and cook for 30 seconds. Add the mussels, pepper flakes, and garlic. Cook for 1 minute. Add the vinho verdo and cook off the alcohol. Add the chicken stock, cover, and bring to a simmer. Continue to simmer until all of the shells open. Transfer the shellfish and broth to a large serving bowl. Season with salt and black pepper. Garnish with parsley, lemon zest, and lemon juice. Drizzle with olive oil. Serve hot with Italian bread for sopping up the broth.

Squid Confit with White Bean Stifado

The Greeks are masters of bean-based stews, which in all their various forms are known as *stifado*. You will often find beans and octopus stifado on the menu as you travel around Greece. That's assuming the place you stop at goes to the trouble of having a menu. Sometimes it's "Do you want grilled fish or octopus?" You can't lose either way. For my stifado, I'm going with squid because it is more sustainable and easier to cook. Instead of the Greek way of grilling squid directly over fire, which can tend to toughness, my confit method is foolproof for tenderness.

serves 4

for the squid confit:

- 1 cup extra virgin olive oil
- 4 cloves garlic
- 2 sprigs thyme
- 2 bay leaves
- Zest and juice of 1 medium lemon
- 1 pound squid, cleaned
- Salt to taste

for the white bean stifado:

- 2 tablespoons olive oil
- 2 cloves garlic
- 1 small onion, diced
- 1 medium carrot, diced
- 1 large rib celery, diced
- 1 cinnamon stick
- ¼ pound dried gigante beans, soaked overnight
- 2 tablespoons white wine
- 1 bay leaf
- 1 sprig thyme
- 2 large tomatoes, chopped
- Juice of ½ large lemon
- 1 tablespoon chopped fresh parsley
- 1 teaspoon chopped fresh oregano
- Salt and fresh ground black pepper to taste

to make the confit:

In a medium stainless steel pot, combine the olive oil, garlic, thyme, bay leaves, lemon zest, and lemon juice. Bring to a simmer. Turn off the heat and add the squid. Let cool at room temperature, cover, and marinate overnight in the refrigerator.

Preheat a grill pan over high heat for 5 minutes. Remove the squid from the oil and pat dry with paper towels. Reserve the oil. Grill the squid until warmed through, about 5 minutes.

to make the stifado:

In a medium pot over medium heat, combine the olive oil, garlic, onion, carrot, celery, and cinnamon stick. Cover and sweat the vegetables until tender, about 10 minutes.

Add the beans, wine, bay leaf, and thyme to the pot. Fill with water to cover. Simmer until the beans are tender, about 1 hour. Add the tomatoes, lemon juice, parsley, oregano, and salt and pepper along with 3 tablespoons of the reserved squid confit oil. Cook until the beans begin to break up a little and the mixture takes on a stewlike consistency, about 30 minutes. Remove and discard the bay leaf and thyme sprig. Top with the squid, and serve hot or cold as a meze.

Seafood Boudin

Old-fashioned boudin—or blood sausage—was once as common in Louisiana as crawfish and beignets. But health concerns rendered the traditional recipe, made with pig's blood, illegal. Guess what? The substitute—made without blood—is pretty darn good, especially when you eat it the traditional way: in your car, parked outside an old-timey filling station/grocery store, with a handful of oyster biscuits, beaucoup hot sauce, and washed down with the traditional beverage of preference . . . an RC Cola. Doesn't hurt to have Dr. John or Etta James blasting on the radio, either. This is a long way of saying that here is my healthier, less-fatty tribute to boudin. Instead of sausage casing, I stuff a fresh, tender squid with chopped shrimp and crab. I suppose a hard-core Creole might have a problem with my calling this a boudin, but it looks like the real thing and you might find that it tastes even better.

serves 4

⅔ cup brown rice

1 gallon + ¾ cup water

¼ pound shrimp (any size), peeled, deveined, and coarsely chopped

¼ pound lump crabmeat, picked over and coarsely chopped

2 teaspoons butter

1 teaspoon Zatarain's Creole Seasoning

½ teaspoon cayenne pepper

1 tablespoon chopped parsley

8 squid bodies

1 tablespoon extra virgin olive oil

Sea salt to taste

Spicy Eggless Mayo

In a large bowl, soak the rice in the 1 gallon of water for 1 hour. Rinse it under running water until the water runs clear.

In a small pot over medium heat, combine the rice with ¾ cup cold water. Bring to a simmer, cover, and cook until all of the water is absorbed, about 25 minutes. Turn off the heat and let the rice sit, covered, for 10 minutes. Remove the cover and fluff the rice with a fork. Set aside to cool.

In a food processor, combine the shrimp, crabmeat, reserved rice, butter, Zatarain's spice, cayenne pepper, and parsley. Pulse until the mixture is the consistency of stuffing at Thanksgiving. Divide the mixture among the squid, stuffing it in and leaving just enough room to seal the ends with toothpicks. Toss the stuffed squid in the olive oil and season with the salt.

Heat a grill pan over high heat until hot. Grill the squid until the filling is heated through, 3 to 4 minutes per side. Serve with the mayo on the side.

Spicy Eggless Mayo

½ teaspoon xanthan gum

1 tablespoon Dijon mustard

1 teaspoon Zatarain's spice

1 teaspoon Tabasco sauce

Juice of ½ large lemon

2 tablespoons white vinegar

1 cup safflower or olive oil

Salt to taste

Pour 1¼ cups water into a blender. While the blender is running on the lowest speed, add the xanthan gum. Blend until it is fully incorporated. Add the mustard, Zatarain's spice, Tabasco, lemon juice, and vinegar and blend until incorporated. With the motor running, slowly add the oil in a thin stream. Season to taste with the salt.

Note: *Xanthan gum, available in health food stores, is a natural organic ingredient that helps give body to many recipes that call for butter, cream, or eggs to thicken a sauce.*

Rock Lobster Tails with Garlic and Oil

Caribbean lobster and true lobster from the Atlantic seaboard are completely different species. Firstly, the Caribbean creature is not really a lobster, but more a crawfish or langouste, and it has no claws. Its meat tends to be a lot firmer and the taste a lot brinier, which is why I chose a gentle poaching method. By bathing the lobster in garlic and olive oil, I keep the flesh tender and allow for some of the sweetness of the lobster to shine through.

serves 4

2 Caribbean rock lobster tails

Sea salt

Juice of 1 large lemon

3 cloves garlic, thinly sliced

1 medium jalapeño chile pepper, seeded and sliced (wear plastic gloves when handling)

6 tablespoons extra virgin olive oil

1 tablespoon chopped fresh basil

Fresh ground black pepper

Slide 2 skewers along the length of each lobster tail and set aside. Bring a large pot of water to a boil. Add enough sea salt so that the water tastes like salt water. Turn off the heat. Slip the lobster tails into the water and let sit for 1 minute. Remove the lobster tails and let cool just enough to handle. Remove the shells and let cool. Remove the skewers from the tails and cut the tails crosswise into 1-inch pieces. Transfer to a medium stainless steel pan. Pour the lemon juice over.

In a small pot, heat the garlic, jalapeño pepper, and oil until a kitchen thermometer reads 190°F. Pour the hot oil over the lobster and let cool until the oil is 120°F on a kitchen thermometer. Place the lobster tails on a platter, drizzle a little of the garlic oil over, and garnish with the basil. Season to taste with salt and black pepper. Serve warm. The lobster will be tender and confitlike, yet still keep its integrity. Serve with a fresh, cool tomato salad for a more substantial bite.

Grilled Octopus Greek Style

I learned this dish from Maria Loi, a Greek chef on the Upper West Side, where she runs her eponymous restaurant LOI, when we worked a charity event together. She called it by its Greek name—*Htapodaki Stin Schara*—but whenever I tried to say that mouthful, it sounded very much like a sneeze. However you say it, though, properly cooked octopus (first braised then grilled) is pure heaven. As for the sauce, *ladolemono* is a Greek version of the lemon and olive oil sauce you find all around the Mediterranean. Mine has mustard powder for extra oomph that might overwhelm other seafood but not a meaty, crusty octopus. It all starts with the octopus—the larger the octopus, the bigger the tentacles, and the bigger the tentacles, the juicier the finished dish!

serves 4

---

4 pounds octopus tentacles

2 cups white wine + more if needed

2 cups red wine + more if needed

10 whole black peppercorns

4 bay leaves

for the ladolemono sauce:

Juice of 2 lemons

Mustard powder to taste

Salt and fresh ground black pepper to taste

1 cup extra virgin olive oil

Chopped chives, for garnish

Preheat the oven to 150°F. In a Dutch oven, combine the octopus tentacles, white wine, red wine, peppercorns, and bay leaves. The tentacles should be completely submerged in the liquid. If not, add more of each wine. Cover the pot and braise until tender, about 6 hours. Remove from the oven and let sit, covered, for 30 minutes.

to make the sauce:

In a jar with a tight-fitting lid, combine the lemon juice, mustard powder, and salt and pepper. Shake vigorously. Add the olive oil and shake again until emulsified.

Preheat a grill pan over high heat until hot. Gently rub just a touch of olive oil on each tentacle, and grill just long enough so that grill marks appear on both sides. Transfer to a plate, spoon some sauce over, and garnish with the chives.

Salmon, Grapefruit, Olive Oil, and Arugula

A few years ago, when I was on a weight-loss program, I read a study that found that grapefruit helps to burn body fat. It came and went as a diet fad, but it did get my attention. About the same time, my friend and fellow chef Rocco Dispirito served a dish at his restaurant, Union Pacific, that included salmon and grapefruit. It blew me away, and this recipe owes much to Rocco. The grapefruit in the accompanying salad lays down a fruit theme, while the arugula adds some bite that contains the big fruit and fish flavors.

serves 4

½ cup sugar

¼ cup kosher salt

2 tablespoons citron vodka

1 tablespoon rice wine vinegar

8 whole shiso leaves

Zest from ½ medium grapefruit

1 salmon fillet (1 pound)

¼ cup baby arugula

2 medium pink grapefruits, sectioned

2 tablespoons shiro soy sauce

Extra virgin olive oil to taste

In a small bowl, combine the sugar, salt, vodka, vinegar, shiso, and grapefruit zest. Rub the mixture all over the salmon and place the salmon in a gallon-size resealable plastic bag. Pat more of the mixture onto the salmon, seal, and let sit at room temperature for 30 to 45 minutes. The salmon will release some liquid. Refrigerate the fish for 4 hours.

Remove the fish from the bag and rinse away the curing mixture. Pat dry with paper towels and, using a very sharp chef's knife, slice the fish width-wise into ¼-inch-thick slices.

Arrange the fish slices on a platter. Place the arugula in a mixing bowl. Add the grapefruit segments, soy sauce, and olive oil and toss to coat. Scatter the greens over the salmon. Spoon the dressing in the bottom of the bowl over the fish and serve immediately.

Grilled Salmon, Lentils, Avocado, and Pecans, with Sherry Vinaigrette

Lentils go well with fat, a fact that was no doubt appreciated by the inventors of the combination of sausage and lentils we find all around the Mediterranean. Why not fatty fish? I asked myself this years ago when I was cooking at Cucina, a sorely missed restaurant in Park Slope, Brooklyn. The answer was, why not? And that's how pan-roasted salmon and lentils found its way into my repertoire. To the healthy fat and flavor of salmon, I have added avocado and pecans with a snappy vinaigrette.

serves 4

for the salmon:

- 4 salmon fillets (6 ounces each), skin on
- 2 tablespoons extra virgin olive oil
- Salt to taste
- Juice of 1 medium lemon
- 1/4 teaspoon cayenne pepper

for the lentil salad:

- 1 cup cooked lentils, at room temperature
- 1 medium avocado, cut into 1/4-inch dice
- 4 cups arugula
- Zest and juice of 1 medium lemon
- 3 tablespoons pecans, toasted
- 2 tablespoons parsley leaves
- Salt and fresh ground black pepper to taste

for the vinaigrette:

- 1/4 cup sherry vinegar
- 1 tablespoon Dijon mustard
- 1 tablespoon finely chopped shallot
- 1 tablespoon honey
- 1/2 cup canola oil or grapeseed oil
- 1 teaspoon tarragon leaves
- Salt and fresh ground black pepper to taste

to make the salmon:

Lightly rub the fish on both sides with the olive oil and season with salt.

Preheat a grill pan over high heat until very hot. Grill the fillets, skin side up, for 2 minutes, then rotate the fish and grill for another 2 minutes. Carefully turn the fish over onto the skin and grill for another 3 to 4 minutes for medium-rare.

Leaving the skin behind on the grill, remove the salmon to a plate and sprinkle with the lemon juice. Season with the cayenne pepper.

to make the lentil salad:

In a medium bowl, toss the lentils, avocado, arugula, lemon zest, lemon juice, pecans, and parsley. Season with salt and black pepper. Transfer to a serving platter and place the salmon over it.

to make the vinaigrette:

In a blender, combine the sherry vinegar, mustard, shallot, and honey. Pulse until thoroughly combined. With the motor running, add the oil in a thin stream, blending until it is emulsified. With the motor running, add the tarragon. Season to taste with salt and black pepper. Drizzle the vinaigrette over the lentil mixture and the fish and serve.

The Five Fat Challenge: Salmon-Avocado Caponata with Pistachios and Black Olive Oil

I first prepared this dish for Dr. Oz. The idea was to incorporate five essential fats in one dish. So here you have salmon, olives, pistachios, canola oil, and avocado, all lifted up the ladder of flavor with a sweet, tart, slightly spicy, and creamy-textured version of caponata—one of my favorite condiments.

serves 4

for the black olive oil:

- 6 black kalamata olives
- 4 black cerignola olives
- ¼ cup extra virgin olive oil

for the caponata:

- 2 tablespoons olive oil
- 1 small onion, diced
- 1 clove garlic, minced
- 1 whole Japanese eggplant (unpeeled), diced
- 1 sprig thyme
- 1 medium yellow squash, diced
- 2 whole plum tomatoes, diced
- 2 tablespoons golden raisins, soaked
- 1 large avocado, diced
- 1 tablespoon chopped parsley
- 1 teaspoon chopped mint
- 1 tablespoon white balsamic vinegar
- Salt and fresh ground black pepper to taste
- Zest of ½ lemon

for the salmon:

- 1 salmon fillet (1½ pounds)
- Salt to taste
- 2 tablespoons canola oil
- Juice of 1 lemon
- Pinch of cayenne pepper
- ¼ cup pistachios, finely grated with a microplane

to make the black olive oil:

In a food processor, combine the kalamata and cerignola olives and the olive oil. Blend until smooth. Let sit for 1 hour to settle.

to make the caponata:

In a small skillet over low heat, warm the olive oil. Add the onion and garlic and sweat until tender, about 5 minutes. Add the eggplant and thyme and increase the heat to medium. Cook until the eggplant is fork-tender, about 5 minutes. Add the squash, tomatoes, and raisins and cook until the mixture begins to break down and come together, about 5 minutes. Add the avocado, parsley, mint, and vinegar, adjust the seasoning with salt and pepper, and cook for 2 minutes to heat the avocado through. Add the lemon zest and stir to combine. Remove and discard the thyme.

to make the salmon:

Preheat the oven to 200°F. Season the salmon with salt and coat thoroughly with the canola oil. Transfer to a nonstick baking sheet. Bake for 8 to 12 minutes. (The fish will look relatively raw and its texture will be tender.) Drizzle the lemon juice over and season with the cayenne. Scatter the pistachios on top.

To serve, place some black olive oil on each of 4 plates and top with some of the caponata. Divide the fish and place on top of the caponata.

Tokyo/Vietnam Tuna Wrap

I am a fan of Vietnamese rice wraps and a big-time sushi lover. This dish combines all of the flavors and textures from both in a neat—as in no mess—package. Even though the tuna is barely cooked, it's important to let it cool so that it doesn't wilt the greens. Make it in advance for hors d'oeuvres. Double the recipe and it's a light summer meal.

serves 4

½ ounce dry vermicelli rice noodles

2 cups warm water

¾ pound sushi-grade yellowfin tuna

1 teaspoon salt

1 tablespoon canola oil

1 avocado

8 large Vietnamese rice paper wrappers

1 cup mizuna or arugula

8 whole mint leaves

8 whole cilantro leaves

for the spicy miso:

1 tablespoon canola oil

2 tablespoons gluten-free white miso

1 tablespoon tamari soy sauce

1 tablespoon sriracha sauce

1 teaspoon Dijon mustard

1 teaspoon sugar in the raw

1 teaspoon fresh ginger juice (see page 16)

1 teaspoon rice wine vinegar

Salt and fresh ground black pepper to taste

In a bowl, soak the rice noodles in the warm water until softened and tender. Thoroughly dry and set aside.

Preheat the grill on medium heat for 5 minutes. Season the tuna with the salt and rub all over with the canola oil. Grill the tuna just long enough to keep it rare on the inside, about 30 seconds per side. Let cool to room temperature.

Slice the tuna crosswise into 1-inch-thick pieces. Cut the pieces in half lengthwise and set aside.

Peel and pit the avocado and quarter it lengthwise. Cut each quarter lengthwise and set aside. Soften the rice paper wrappers one at a time by submerging them in a bowl of chilled water for 10 seconds. Transfer to a nonstick surface in a single layer. Have a damp cloth ready.

To make the rolls, prepare them one at a time by placing 1 wrapper directly on top of another. Arrange one-eighth of the rice noodles, tuna, avocado, mizuna or arugula, mint, and cilantro down the center of the wrapper. Roll the wrappers like an egg roll, tucking in the sides as you go. Place on an oiled piece of plastic wrap and cover with the damp cloth.

to make the miso:

In a blender, combine the canola oil, miso, tamari, sriracha, mustard, sugar, ginger juice, and vinegar. Blend on medium speed until smooth and the consistency of mayonnaise. Season with salt and pepper. The sauce will keep covered in the refrigerator for up to 7 days.

To serve, slice each roll crosswise into 3 pieces and serve the sauce on the side.

Grilled Spanish Mackerel with Black Olives, Tomatoes, and Pistou

Mackerel is so full flavored it can stand up to the most powerful ingredients. It is often stewed or braised with olives and tomatoes. I wanted to keep the pure flavor of grilled mackerel, so I saved the vegetables, herbs, and seasonings that are usually used in the stew for a separate salad. I top the fish instead with a traditional pistou—the basil- and garlic-infused olive oil dressing of Provence.

serves 4

for the fish:

- 1/4 cup extra virgin olive oil
- Juice of 1/2 lemon
- 4 Spanish mackerel fillets (5 ounces each)
- Salt to taste

for the salad:

- 1 cup multicolored cherry tomatoes, halved
- 2 chopped kalamata olives
- 2 tablespoons whole parsley leaves
- 1 tablespoon whole celery leaves
- 1/2 teaspoon red-pepper flakes
- 1 teaspoon lemon zest
- Juice of 1/2 lemon
- 2 tablespoons extra virgin olive oil

for the pistou:

- 1/4 cup extra virgin olive oil
- 2 tablespoons chopped fresh basil
- 1 clove garlic, minced
- Salt and fresh ground black pepper to taste

to make the fish:

Preheat a cast-iron grill pan over medium heat for 5 minutes. In a small bowl, combine the olive oil and lemon juice and rub all over the mackerel. Season with salt. Grill the fish until it flakes easily, about 2 1/2 minutes per side. Transfer to a plate and cover to keep warm.

to make the salad:

In a medium bowl, combine the tomatoes, olives, parsley, celery leaves, pepper flakes, lemon zest, lemon juice, and olive oil. Toss to thoroughly incorporate. Set aside.

to make the pistou:

In a blender, combine the olive oil, basil, garlic, and salt and black pepper. Blend until smooth.

To serve, scatter the tomato mixture over the fish and serve the pistou on the side.

Tuna Cubes with Citrus Soy, Chives, and Cucumber

This tuna salad is one of the most successful items I ever put on a menu. In 2½ years, I sold 62,000 orders! I think the public was trying to tell me something, and I'd like to pass it on to you. I've streamlined it a bit and lightened the flavors, but the idea of cubes of hand-cut tuna in a tangy, sweet, and savory dressing is still at the heart of this recipe. It's the same flavor principle that works so well in beef tartare (see page 107), but with more of an Asian accent.

serves 4

2 Persian cucumbers, thinly sliced

2 teaspoons rice wine vinegar

1 teaspoon superfine sugar

Sea salt to taste

1 pound sushi-grade tuna, cut into ½-inch cubes

4 tablespoons citrus soy sauce (ponzu)

1 tablespoon finely chopped chives

2 tablespoons olive oil

In a small bowl, combine the cucumbers, vinegar, sugar, and sea salt. Set aside for 10 minutes.

Meanwhile, in a medium bowl, combine the tuna and ponzu sauce and toss to coat. Using a slotted spoon, transfer the cucumbers to the bowl. Add the chives and toss to distribute evenly. Drizzle with the olive oil and serve cold.

Note: Use the best sushi-grade yellowfin tuna you can find. I never use the endangered bluefin tuna, and I urge you not to either. These magnificent animals can grow to 1,000 pounds, are as warm-blooded as mammals, and can knife through the water at 70 miles per hour. Sadly, they have taken quite a beating as more and more of the world turns on to the sushi craze. Whenever you order tuna in a restaurant, ask what kind it is. You want yellowfin, not the endangered bluefin. If they don't know the answer, don't order it.

Mackerel, Oranges, Mint, Chiles, and Lemon Agrumato

Mackerel is an overlooked treasure. When they are running along the coast of New Jersey and New York in the spring and fall, there are acres and acres of them just off-shore. Like salmon, they are a fatty fish, full of omega-3s, and take well to citrus, which cuts through the fat and refreshes your palate. Unlike salmon, they are inexpensive. Mackerel must be fresh because the delicious oils in their flesh get rancid very quickly. My dressing is based on agrumato, which is a lemon-infused olive oil made in Abruzzo, Italy, where hand-harvested olives and fresh-picked citrus are put through the same press. It's a very special flavor that can't be duplicated, so I recommend that you seek it out in gourmet stores or markets specializing in Italian food. A flavorful cold-pressed extra virgin olive oil is a good pinch hitter.

serves 4

---

1 Cara Cara orange

1 pound sushi-grade Spanish mackerel fillet

1 red jalapeño chile pepper, seeded and sliced paper thin (wear plastic gloves when handling)

2 tablespoons shiro soy sauce

Juice of 1/2 lemon

12 sprigs mint, torn into pieces

Sea salt to taste

3 tablespoons agrumato or cold-pressed extra virgin olive oil

Section the orange, removing the pith and membrane over a bowl to catch the juices. Using a sharp knife, slice the fish into 1/4-inch-thick slices crosswise. Arrange the slices on a serving platter and scatter the jalapeño pepper over. Splash the soy sauce, lemon juice, and orange juice all over the fish, followed by the mint and the orange sections. Season lightly with the sea salt and drizzle with the agrumato.

Olive Oil–Poached Cod with Roasted Tomato and Peppers

Did you ever wonder why Mediterranean cuisine features so much cod when there is not a cod to be found between Gibraltar and the coast of Lebanon? Intrepid sailors in the late Middle Ages found the seemingly endless supply of cod off the coast of North America, and it became a staple of Mediterranean cuisine. Usually it is used in its dried, salted form, but I found that gently poaching cod in fresh olive oil and serving it with a stew of tomatoes and peppers produces a fish with delicate textures and a less salty, "fishy" flavor. Don't be concerned about the amount of olive oil I use here. You can always fry a few potatoes in it, which will remove any impurities and fishy taste, and then store it in the fridge to reuse for any recipe that calls for cooking in olive oil.

Cod is endangered in many areas, particularly in New England. Ask your fish source where it came from and if it's sustainable.

serves 4

for the cod:

2½ cups warm water

¼ cup salt

4 cod fillets (6 ounces each)

1 quart olive oil

Zest of 1 lemon

2 sprigs thyme

3 cloves garlic, gently crushed

Extra virgin olive oil, for serving

for the roasted tomatoes:

4 plum tomatoes, halved

2 tablespoons extra virgin olive oil

1 tablespoon balsamic vinegar

1 sprig thyme

1 clove garlic, thinly sliced

Sea salt to taste

Fresh ground black pepper to taste

2 tablespoons whole parsley leaves

for the peppers:

1 tablespoon extra virgin olive oil

2 red bell peppers, thinly sliced

1 small yellow onion, thinly sliced

Salt and fresh ground black pepper to taste

to brine the cod:

In a large pot, combine the warm water with the salt, stir until dissolved, and chill. Submerge the fish in the brine and let sit for 30 minutes.

to make the tomatoes:

Preheat the oven to 450°F. Line a baking sheet with parchment paper. In a medium bowl, combine the tomatoes with the olive oil, vinegar, thyme, garlic, sea salt, and black pepper and toss to coat. Arrange in a single layer on the baking sheet and roast until the tomatoes are charred and the skins slip off easily, 20 to 25 minutes. Remove the skins and toss the tomatoes with the parsley. Set aside.

(continued on page 88)

to make the peppers:

In a medium skillet over medium-high heat, warm the olive oil until hot. Add the peppers and cook, stirring frequently, until they get some color, about 5 minutes. Add the onion and cook, stirring frequently, until the onion and peppers are tender, about 25 minutes. Season with salt and black pepper. Add to the tomato mixture and toss.

to assemble the cod:

Remove the cod from the brine and pat dry. In a large pot, combine the olive oil, lemon zest, thyme, and garlic and heat to 120°F on a kitchen thermometer. Working in batches, gently slide the fish into the pot so that it is covered entirely with the oil; if not, baste frequently. Poach the fish until just cooked through, 20 to 25 minutes. Arrange a fillet on each of 4 plates, spoon the tomato mixture over, and drizzle with olive oil.

Grilled Sea Bass with Spigarello, Chiles, and Garlic

Black American sea bass is, in my opinion, one of the best eating fish in the ocean. Although it is more common these days, it is not available in every fish market (except in Chinese markets, where they prize their fresh fish!). You can also catch your own. Its sweet flesh is succulent, and stands up to several cooking methods including grilling, which is the way we cooked its Mediterranean look-alike when I worked at the Hotel Siranuse on the Amalfi coast. Every morning I would show up at the docks with my wheelbarrow and buy fish straight off the boat. The chef, Marco, was a dapper guy and a master with a wood-fired grill, where he did whole fish like these on the bone and served them with spigarello, a cousin of broccoli rabe. Couldn't be simpler or better. My only change here is to make things a little easier by cooking fillets. If you feel like cooking the fish whole, you won't be disappointed. Serve with Quinoa, Beet, and Arugula Salad (see page 37).

serves 4

4 sea bass fillets (6 ounces each), skin on
Kosher salt to taste

4 tablespoons extra virgin olive oil, divided
Juice of 1 lemon

4 cloves garlic, thinly sliced

2 fresh Thai red chile peppers, chopped (wear plastic gloves when handling)

1 pound spigarello or broccoli rabe, cut into 2-inch pieces
Salt to taste

Prepare a charcoal grill or preheat a gas grill. Season the fish with kosher salt and rub 1 tablespoon of the olive oil all over it. Place the fish on the grill skin side down and grill for 3 minutes. Turn and grill until the flesh turns white and flakes easily, about 2 minutes. Transfer to a warmed plate and drizzle 1 tablespoon of the olive oil and the lemon juice over it.

Meanwhile, in a large skillet over medium-high heat, warm the remaining 2 tablespoons olive oil until it shimmers. Add the garlic and red chile peppers and cook, stirring frequently, until fragrant, about 1 minute. Add the spigarello or broccoli rabe and cook, stirring frequently, for 3 minutes, or until just tender. Season with salt.

To serve, place the fish on top of the spigarello or broccoli rabe and serve.

Grilled Sea Bream with Lemon Gremolata and Spinach

Sea bream, also known as orata or dourade, is ideal for grilling or poaching. It has sweet, delicate white flesh and a size and thickness that doesn't challenge most home cooks who worry about drying out their fish or, on the other hand, undercooking it. Stuffing the fish with aromatics, then serving it with a slightly sweetened gremolata, lends the subtly flavored flesh a complex and full flavor. Our East Coast porgy works well with this, or a good-size, pumpkin-shaped panfish from a southern or midwestern pond would also do just fine. If purchasing at the fish counter, ask your fishmonger to gut and scale the fish.

serves 4

for the gremolata:

Zest of 2 lemons + juice of 1

1 teaspoon superfine sugar

½ teaspoon salt

2 tablespoons boiling water

1 tablespoon olive oil

1 tablespoon parsley leaves

1 tablespoon whole mint leaves

for the sea bream:

2 cloves garlic, thinly sliced

2 sprigs thyme

2 sea bream (1½ pounds each), gutted and scaled

Juice of 1 lemon

2 tablespoons olive oil

Salt and fresh ground black pepper to taste

for the spinach:

2 tablespoons olive oil

2 cloves garlic, thinly sliced

½ teaspoon red-pepper flakes

1 pound spinach, cleaned

Salt to taste

to make the gremolata:

In a small heatproof bowl, combine the lemon zest, lemon juice, sugar, and salt. Set aside for 15 to 20 minutes to macerate. Add the boiling water and blanch the zest for 3 minutes. Strain the liquid from the zest and transfer the zest to a small bowl. Add the olive oil, parsley, and mint and stir to combine. Set aside.

to make the sea bream:

Prepare a charcoal grill or preheat a gas grill for 15 minutes. Meanwhile, divide the garlic and thyme between the fish and stuff in the cavities. Drizzle the lemon juice over and rub all over with the olive oil. Season with salt and black pepper. Grill the fish until the flesh is opaque and pulls away from the bones easily, about 4 to 5 minutes per side.

to make the spinach:

Heat the olive oil in a medium skillet over medium-high heat. Add the garlic and cook, stirring, until fragrant, about 1 minute. Add the pepper flakes and cook, stirring frequently, until fragrant, about 30 seconds. Add the spinach and cook, stirring frequently, until wilted and tender. Season with the salt.

To serve, remove the garlic and thyme from the fish cavities and top with the gremolata. Arrange over the spinach.

Grilled Striped Bass with Sweet Peppers, New Potatoes, and Pesto

The majestic striper is king of the game fish in the Northeast. Although overfishing has taken its toll in recent years, I think it's okay to catch and cook one or two each year. If you do pull in one of these beauties, do it the honor of a real wood fire. It adds an extra bit of smoky pungency that is incomparable. You can readily find farmed stripers of just the right size in many fish markets. If you live in the Southeast, where there are no stripers, fresh-caught snapper will do, or even redfish. If you are not an angler, make friends with some and invite them over for dinner as long as they promise to share their catch.

serves 4

for the peppers and potatoes:

- 2 red bell peppers, seeded and cut into ¼-inch-thick slices
- ½ pound new potatoes, quartered
- 1 onion, thinly sliced
- 2 tablespoons olive oil
- 1 teaspoon lemon juice
- ½ teaspoon cayenne pepper
- Salt and fresh ground black pepper to taste

for the pesto:

- ¼ cup pine nuts, toasted
- ¼ cup finely grated Parmesan cheese
- 3 tablespoons olive oil
- 1 teaspoon lemon juice
- ¼ cup fresh basil, cut into thin ribbons
- ¼ cup fresh parsley, cut into thin ribbons

for the fish:

- 4 striped bass fillets (6 ounces each), at least 1 inch thick, skin on, bones removed
- 2 tablespoons extra virgin olive oil
- Kosher salt and fresh ground black pepper to taste
- Juice of 1 lemon

to make the peppers and potatoes:

Prepare a charcoal grill or preheat a gas grill. In a medium bowl, combine the peppers, potatoes, onion, olive oil, lemon juice, cayenne pepper, and salt and black pepper and toss to coat. Wrap in foil and place on the upper rack of the grill. Cover and cook until fork-tender, about 45 minutes. Set aside in the foil to keep warm.

to make the pesto:

In a small bowl, combine the pine nuts, cheese, olive oil, lemon juice, basil, and parsley and stir to mix thoroughly. Set aside.

to make the fish:

Rub the fish all over with the olive oil. Season with the kosher salt and black pepper and place skin side down on the grill. Grill for 3 minutes, then gently turn, making sure not to lose the skin. Grill for 3 minutes.

In a bowl, combine the peppers and potatoes with 1 tablespoon of the pesto. Toss to coat. Arrange the fish on a serving plate, drizzle with lemon juice, and serve with the peppers and potatoes and the remaining pesto on the side.

Broiled Local Flounder Oreganata with Charred Broccoli

When I was younger, my mom would put a fillet of flounder or sole on a piece of foil. She would drizzle olive oil, lemon juice, and bread crumbs on top and bake it *to death* in the oven. Now that I have some years behind a stove, I have discovered that flounder is so delicate that it doesn't need to be subdued by long cooking. Like chicken, it goes well with many different ingredients and flavors. This combination is my heartfelt tribute to Mom. Serve with Blistered Broccoli with Garlic and Chiles (see page 131).

serves 4

---

4 flounder fillets (6 ounces each)

4 tablespoons olive oil, divided

Juice of 2 lemons

2 cloves garlic, minced

1 shallot, finely chopped

1 cup Italian bread crumbs

2 tablespoons chopped fresh parsley

2 tablespoons chopped fresh oregano

2 tablespoons grated Parmesan cheese

1 tablespoon sea salt

½ teaspoon fresh ground black pepper

¼ teaspoon cayenne pepper

½ cup white wine

Blistered Broccoli with Garlic and Chiles (page 131)

Coat the fillets all over with 2 tablespoons of the olive oil and place on a nonstick baking sheet. Drizzle half of the lemon juice over the fish. Set aside.

Preheat the broiler.

In a small bowl, toss together the garlic, shallot, bread crumbs, parsley, oregano, cheese, sea salt, black pepper, and cayenne pepper. Distribute the mixture evenly over the fish. Drizzle with the white wine, followed by the remaining 2 tablespoons olive oil.

Place the fish on the middle rack below the broiler. Broil until the crust is golden and the fish flakes apart, 7 to 10 minutes, depending on the thickness of the fillets. Arrange on a plate, drizzle some lemon juice over, and serve with the broccoli.

CHAPTER 5

POULTRY AND MEAT

One of the most remarkable changes in the world's diet has taken place in the last 50 years. As more and more nations move toward developed economies, people tend to want more poultry and meat in their diets. This transformation is called the "nutrition transition." Hand in hand with this change, the rate of obesity in the world has gone up tremendously. Does that mean that Buffalo chicken wings and steaks are the culprits? Not necessarily. During this same time, people around the world have begun to consume more sugary drinks and millions of tons of french fries, both loaded with calories. I think it's safe to say that people crave meat because it is such an efficient source of energy and protein. These are good things. Meat is also a source of fat. Again, not necessarily bad. The problem, according to many studies, is saturated fat. Although free-range animals that are allowed to forage and graze on their natural diets are high in polyunsaturated fat and monounsaturated fat, there's no getting away from the fact that all land animals have some saturated fat. My solution to a love of poultry and meat, on the one hand, and a desire to eat healthy, on the other, is to eat meat occasionally (once or twice a week) and—this is critical—in *smaller* portions. No one needs a 1-pound steak or an 8-ounce hamburger. Servings of 4 to 6 ounces will satisfy and nourish you. Think of meat as an accent or an important guest star in the cast of characters in your diet, and enjoy it when you have it, just not every day.

Slow-Roasted Organic Chicken with Parsley, Sage, Rosemary, and Thyme   98

Grilled Chicken with Tomato Jam   100

Grilled Chicken with Ramp Pesto   101

Barbecue Chicken Wraps with Celery and Bean Sprouts   104

Almond-Dusted Chicken Breasts   105

Grilled Turkey, Avocado, and Tomato on Seven Grain   106

Beef Tartare with Capers, Pistachio Pesto, and Watermelon-Tomato Salad   107

Grilled Skirt Steak with Warm Potato Salad and Chimichurri   110

Baby Lamb Chops with Chili, Mint, and Provençal Marinade   111

Oven-Roasted Lamb Shoulder   112

Chorizo and Chickpeas with Charred Onions, Black Olives, and Herbs   115

Slow-Roasted Organic Chicken with Parsley, Sage, Rosemary, and Thyme

My inspiration for this recipe, predictable from its title, is the Simon and Garfunkel song "Scarborough Fair." My other influence is Provençal cooking, or what is typically referred to as "the Cuisine of the Sun"—lots of herbs, garlic, and olive oil.

serves 4

2 tablespoons extra virgin olive oil

1 tablespoon paprika

1 tablespoon sea salt

1 teaspoon garlic powder

1 organic roasting chicken (3½ to 4 pounds)

½ cup whole parsley

½ cup whole sage

½ cup whole rosemary

½ cup whole thyme

1 lemon, quartered

4 cloves garlic

2 shallots, chopped

Preheat the oven to 450°F. In a small bowl, mix the olive oil, paprika, sea salt, and garlic powder into a paste and rub it liberally on the inside and outside of the chicken. Stuff the cavity of the chicken with the parsley, sage, rosemary, thyme, lemon, garlic, and shallots. Truss the chicken.

Set the chicken on a roasting rack in a roasting pan and roast until the juices run clear and the internal temperature of the bird at its thickest part (the thigh) is 165°F, about 50 to 60 minutes. Remove the pan from the oven and baste the chicken with the juices that have collected on the bottom of the pan. Let rest 15 minutes. Present the bird whole to the table for a beautiful family-style presentation or cut it into 8 pieces before serving.

Grilled Chicken with Tomato Jam

This originated as a panini served with arugula, fresh mozzarella, pesto, and tomato jam. Then I turned it into a pasta topping. Then I took out the pasta and tossed the pesto with rice. Then I took out the rice, leaving the chicken along with the tomato jam and finished with pesto drizzled on the plate. I chose parsley for the pesto here because you get a lot of herbal flavor in the chicken already, and parsley cuts through it all for a nice balance among all these strong flavors.

serves 4

for the chicken:

- 4 chicken breasts
- ¼ cup olive oil
- 2 cloves garlic, sliced
- 2 shallots, sliced
- 4 sprigs thyme
- 4 sprigs rosemary
- Sea salt to taste

for the jam:

- 1 cup canned peeled Italian plum tomatoes, quartered
- 1 teaspoon tomato paste
- 1 teaspoon extra virgin olive oil
- 1 clove garlic
- ¼ teaspoon red-pepper flakes
- Pinch of sugar
- Salt to taste

for the pesto:

- ½ cup parsley, stems removed, finely chopped
- 3 tablespoons extra virgin olive oil
- 2 tablespoons grated Parmesan cheese
- 2 tablespoons pine nuts, toasted, coarsely chopped
- ½ clove garlic, smashed into a fine paste
- 1 teaspoon lemon juice
- Salt and fresh ground black pepper to taste

to make the chicken:

Butterfly the chicken by placing a breast flat side down on a cutting board and using a sharp knife to cut width-wise three-quarters of the way through. Open the breast like a book and gently stroke the opening with your knife until both sides are equal. Repeat with the remaining breasts. In a shallow dish, combine the olive oil, garlic, shallots, thyme, and rosemary. Add the chicken and marinate in the refrigerator for at least 20 minutes or up to 24 hours.

to make the jam:

In a 1-quart saucepan, combine the tomatoes, tomato paste, olive oil, garlic, pepper flakes, sugar, and salt. Cover and cook over low heat until thickened to a jam consistency, about 2 hours. Let cool at room temperature for 30 minutes before transferring to the refrigerator. The jam will store, covered in the refrigerator, for about 2 weeks.

to make the pesto:

In a medium bowl, combine the parsley, olive oil, cheese, pine nuts, garlic, lemon juice, and salt and black pepper. Set aside.

Prepare a charcoal grill or preheat a gas grill. Remove the chicken from the marinade and season with the sea salt. Grill until a thermometer inserted in the thickest portion registers 165°F and the juices run clear, 4 to 5 minutes per side. To serve, top the chicken with the tomato jam and some pesto.

Grilled Chicken with Ramp Pesto

Ramps, if you are not familiar with them, are a kind of wild onion that grows on riverbanks in the spring when the morels are popping and the shad are coming up the rivers. They are the first promise of warmer days and fresh fruits and vegetables to come. Making pesto with them gives it a blast of oniony sharpness that wakes up your palate big-time. Because ramps are so sharp, this pesto calls for pistachios for their buttery sweetness (instead of the less assertive pine nuts traditionally used in pesto). Serve this on the Grilled Chicken (opposite) with Blistered Broccoli with Garlic and Chiles (see page 131) or Peppers Stewed in Olive Oil, Herbs, and Garlic (see page 124). Or, put the chicken breast between 2 slices of ciabatta and brush with the pesto.

makes about 1½ cups

2 tablespoons salt, divided

8 ramps, stems removed, washed

½ cup finely grated Parmesan cheese

1 cup pistachios, toasted

3 tablespoons extra virgin olive oil

Juice of ½ lemon

Salt and fresh ground black pepper to taste

Fill a medium bowl with ice, water, and 1 tablespoon of salt. Bring a medium pot of water to a boil. Add 1 tablespoon of salt and return to a boil. Add the ramps and cook for 1 minute. Remove the ramps and immediately place in the ice water. After 2 minutes, remove the ramps and drain off any excess water. In a food processor, combine the ramps, cheese, pistachios, olive oil, lemon juice, and salt and pepper. Pulse until combined. Taste and adjust by adding more olive oil if the flavor is too sharp.

Grilled Chicken
with Ramp Pesto

Barbecue Chicken Wraps with Celery and Bean Sprouts

This is a case of East meets Southwest: the flavors and textures of the famous Vietnamese Ban Mi sandwich wrapped up in a tortilla. Mixing spicy sriracha and hoisin is purely Far East, but the result is very evocative of American barbecue sauce. I guess it goes to show you that many cultures can take different routes to produce the same effect on your palate.

serves 4

for the chicken:

- 4 tablespoons olive oil
- 2 cloves garlic, sliced
- 2 shallots, sliced
- 4 sprigs thyme
- 4 boneless, skinless chicken breasts (6 ounces each)
- Sea salt and fresh ground black pepper to taste

for the glaze:

- 2 tablespoons sriracha sauce
- 6 tablespoons hoisin sauce

for the wraps:

- 4 brown rice or whole wheat tortillas
- 2 ribs celery, cut into matchsticks
- 1 carrot, cut into matchsticks
- 1 cup bean sprouts

to make the chicken:

In a shallow dish, combine the olive oil, garlic, shallots, and thyme. Add the chicken and marinate for at least 20 minutes or up to 24 hours.

to make the glaze:

In a small bowl, whisk together the sriracha and hoisin. Set aside.

Prepare a charcoal grill or preheat a gas grill. Remove the chicken from the marinade and season with the sea salt and pepper. Grill until a thermometer inserted in the thickest portion registers 165°F and the juices run clear, 4 to 5 minutes per side. Brush the chicken with the sriracha mixture and grill for 1 minute longer. Turn over and repeat. Transfer to a cutting board and cut into slices.

to make the wraps:

Warm the tortillas by placing them on the grill for 30 seconds, turning them over halfway through. Arrange equal parts of chicken on each tortilla, top with the celery, carrot, and bean sprouts, and roll up, tucking in the sides as you go. Serve whole or cut in half and wrapped in foil to keep warm.

Almond-Dusted Chicken Breasts

Like most kids, my son went through a phase of wanting to eat only one thing. That thing was McDonald's Chicken McNuggets. The only problem is they are coated in flour, and he has a problem with gluten. So I started to experiment with different mixes of flours and pulverized nuts. Almonds are a great alternative to bread crumbs; not only are they deeply flavorful, but they have a top-notch nutrition profile. My boy liked this with amaranth flour, but I think you'll find that almonds do the trick. This recipe calls for sorghum flour. This sweet, nutty grain is commonly used to feed live-stock. It is high in protein, and gluten-free.

serves 4

2 pounds boneless, skinless chicken breasts

½ cup sorghum flour, divided

2 eggs, beaten

2 tablespoons water

1 tablespoon kosher salt

½ cup almonds, blanched, finely chopped

2 sprigs thyme, picked and chopped

Salt and fresh ground black pepper to taste

6 tablespoons canola oil

2 cloves garlic

Butterfly the chicken by placing a breast flat side down on a cutting board and using a sharp knife to cut width-wise three-quarters of the way through. Open the breast like a book and gently stroke the opening with your knife until both sides are equal. Repeat with the remaining breasts. Place all but 2 tablespoons of the sorghum flour on a plate. In a shallow bowl, whisk together the eggs, water, and the salt. On a plate, mix the remaining 2 tablespoons sorghum flour with the almonds and thyme. Season the chicken with the salt and pepper and coat lightly with the sorghum flour, followed by the egg mixture and the almond mixture.

In a large skillet over medium heat, warm the canola oil until it ripples. Slip the chicken into the pan and fry until it's golden brown and a thermometer inserted in the thickest portion registers 165°F, about 4 minutes per side. Add the garlic to the pan and allow the flavor to permeate the chicken breasts for 1 minute. Remove the chicken from the skillet and serve.

Grilled Turkey, Avocado, and Tomato on Seven Grain

I don't know why it is that people grill chicken and make wonderful sandwiches with it, but when it comes to turkey, they make do with the lifeless shrink-wrapped product found in the deli case at the supermarket. Turkey breast is easy to grill when you slice it into cutlets. Buy a good heritage breed for full flavor. Avocado gives this sandwich the creamy mouth feel of mayonnaise. Arugula dressed with a mildly spicy vinaigrette that pumps up the flavor adds a sharp and tangy finish.

serves 4

for the turkey:

- ¼ cup olive oil
- 2 cloves garlic, sliced
- 2 shallots, sliced
- 4 sprigs thyme
- 4 sprigs rosemary
- 1 boneless, skinless turkey breast (about 1½ pounds), sliced into 4 cutlets
- 4 ounces arugula
- 2 beefsteak tomatoes, sliced width-wise into 8 slices
- Sea salt to taste
- 8 slices seven-grain bread, toasted
- 1 avocado, quartered and thinly sliced

for the avocado puree:

- 1 avocado, pitted and halved
- 1 teaspoon extra virgin olive oil
- 1 teaspoon lemon juice
- ¼ teaspoon cayenne pepper
- Salt to taste

for the vinaigrette:

- 1 teaspoon extra virgin olive oil
- 1 teaspoon balsamic vinegar
- Salt and fresh ground black pepper to taste

to make the turkey:

In a shallow dish, combine the olive oil, garlic, shallots, thyme, and rosemary. Add the turkey cutlets and turn to coat. Cover and marinate in the refrigerator overnight.

to make the avocado puree:

In a food processor, combine the avocado halves, olive oil, lemon juice, cayenne pepper, and salt. Process until the mixture is the consistency of mayonnaise.

to make the vinaigrette:

In a small bowl, whisk together the olive oil and vinegar. Season with the salt and black pepper. In a bowl, combine the arugula and tomatoes. Add the dressing and toss to coat.

Remove the turkey from the marinade and season with sea salt. Prepare a charcoal grill or preheat a gas grill. Grill the cutlets until they are no longer pink inside, about 4 to 5 minutes per side. Spread 4 slices of the toast with the avocado puree. Place a turkey cutlet on each. Top with the avocado slices, the arugula mixture, and the remaining bread. Cut the sandwiches in half diagonally and serve.

Beef Tartare with Capers, Pistachio Pesto, and Watermelon-Tomato Salad

Beef tartare is one of my favorite recipes. The combination of flavors and textures is super complex. As a chef, I take that as a challenge to try to do something new. A pesto based on pistachio gives you all the creaminess that you get from egg in the classic recipe, but the flavor is so much more interesting. Likewise, old-school tartare relies on croutons for crunch, but I opt for fresh watermelon and sliced fennel. All in all, very unusual but very harmonious. Sure it has beef, but in the right amounts, beef is delicious, nourishing, and the saturated fat is negligible and well balanced by the pistachios and olive oil.

Freshness is very important in this recipe. Don't be put off by the list of ingredients. If you lay them out in little dishes, it all comes together quickly. The end result always impresses.

serves 4

for the beef tartare:

- 1 tablespoon anchovy paste
- 1 teaspoon Dijon mustard
- 4 dashes Worcestershire sauce
- 4 dashes Tabasco sauce
- 1 tablespoon extra virgin olive oil
- 1 pound freshly ground or diced filet mignon
- 1 tablespoon capers in brine, rinsed
- 1 tablespoon finely chopped cornichons
- 1 tablespoon finely chopped shallot
- 1 tablespoon finely chopped chives
- 2 teaspoons finely chopped parsley
- 1 teaspoon finely chopped jalapeño chile pepper (wear plastic gloves when handling)
- Salt and fresh ground black pepper to taste

for the pesto:

- 2 tablespoons chopped pistachios
- 2 tablespoons chopped fresh parsley
- 2 tablespoons chopped fresh basil
- 2 tablespoons grated Parmesan cheese
- 2 tablespoons extra virgin olive oil
- 1 clove garlic, minced

for the salad:

- ¼ cup diced watermelon
- ¼ cup cherry tomatoes, halved
- ¼ cup thinly sliced fennel
- 1 tablespoon chopped fresh parsley
- 2 tablespoons extra virgin olive oil
- 1 teaspoon white balsamic vinegar
- Sea salt and fresh ground black pepper to taste

(continued on page 108)

to make the beef tartare:

Set a medium bowl in a large bowl filled with ice. In the medium bowl, whisk the anchovy paste, mustard, Worcestershire sauce, Tabasco sauce, and olive oil into a paste. Stir in the meat, capers, cornichons, shallot, chives, parsley, jalapeño pepper, and salt and black pepper. Chill in the refrigerator.

to make the pesto:

In a food processor, combine the pistachios, parsley, basil, cheese, olive oil, and garlic. Pulse until smooth.

to make the salad:

In a small bowl, combine the watermelon, tomatoes, fennel, parsley, olive oil, vinegar, and sea salt and black pepper. Toss to combine thoroughly.

Serve the steak tartare in the center of each plate, drizzle the pesto around it, and spoon some watermelon-tomato salad on the side.

Grilled Skirt Steak with Warm Potato Salad and Chimichurri

I serve this eminently grillable cut (because it is so well marbled) with chimichurri, the traditional condiment of Argentine gauchos. Skirt steak—even from grain-fed cattle—has the wild flavor that you get from grass-fed beef, so this is as close as you are going to get to the Argentine experience, unless you have a grass-fed supplier (which is getting more and more common). By the way, grass-fed beef has a different—some experts say healthier—fat profile than corn-fed animals.

serves 4

for the skirt steak:

- ¼ cup olive oil
- 2 cloves garlic, thinly sliced
- 2 shallots, sliced
- 4 sprigs thyme
- Sea salt and fresh ground black pepper to taste
- 4 skirt steaks (6 ounces each)

for the potatoes:

- 16 small red bliss potatoes
- Salt to taste

for the chimichurri:

- 1 cup finely chopped fresh parsley leaves
- ½ cup extra virgin olive oil
- 2 tablespoons red wine vinegar
- 2 tablespoons finely chopped fresh oregano leaves
- 3 cloves garlic, minced
- ½ teaspoon red-pepper flakes
- Salt and fresh ground black pepper to taste

to make the skirt steak:

In a shallow dish, combine the olive oil, garlic, shallots, thyme, and sea salt and black pepper. Add the steaks and turn to coat. Cover and marinate in the refrigerator overnight. Remove from the marinade and drain the excess oil.

to make the potatoes:

Place the potatoes in a medium pot and add water to cover. Add salt and bring to a boil. Cook until fork-tender, about 25 minutes. Drain. When cool enough to handle, cut the potatoes in half. Transfer to a serving bowl and set aside.

to make the chimichurri:

In a small bowl, whisk together the parsley, olive oil, vinegar, oregano, garlic, pepper flakes, and salt and black pepper. Pour half of the sauce over the potatoes and toss to coat. Set aside.

Prepare a charcoal grill or preheat a gas grill for 15 minutes. Season the skirt steak with salt and black pepper. Grill until a thermometer inserted in the center registers 145°F for medium-rare, about 4 minutes per side. Transfer to a cutting board to rest for 5 minutes. Serve topped with the chimichurri sauce and the potatoes on the side.

Baby Lamb Chops with Chili, Mint, and Provençal Marinade

Loin chops are the only cut I like for lamb chops. If you look at one, you'll see it's like a mini-porterhouse, offering a combination of filet and loin, a beautiful choice of textures. In Italy, *scottadito*—baby lamb—is often prepared with lemon, mint, and chili, which is how my girlfriend and I first had it at the gorgeous Hotel Vittoria overlooking the Bay of Naples.

Store the remaining chili oil in an airtight container in the refrigerator for up to 3 months. It can be used to give a little heat to chicken, pork, vegetables, and salads.

serves 4

for the marinade:

- ½ cup extra virgin olive oil
- 3 cloves garlic, sliced
- 3 shallots, sliced
- 2 sprigs rosemary
- 2 sprigs thyme
- 1 teaspoon red-pepper flakes
- 1 teaspoon salt

for the lamb:

- 8 lamb loin chops
- 1 teaspoon sea salt + additional to taste
- 1 teaspoon fresh ground black pepper
- Juice of 2 lemons
- 2 sprigs mint

for the chili oil:

- 3 cups olive oil
- 2 tablespoons red-pepper flakes

to make the marinade:

In a gallon resealable plastic bag, combine the olive oil, garlic, shallots, rosemary, thyme, pepper flakes, and salt.

to make the lamb:

Add the lamb chops to the plastic bag, seal, and marinate overnight in the refrigerator.

to make the chili oil:

Meanwhile, in a small saucepan, combine the olive oil and pepper flakes and bring to a simmer over low heat. Set aside to cool, then strain. Refrigerate until ready to use.

Bring the lamb chops to room temperature. Preheat the broiler with the rack 4 inches from the heat source. Remove the lamb chops from the marinade and scrape away any of the marinade bits that have stuck to the meat. Season with the sea salt and black pepper and place on a broiler pan. Broil for about 3 minutes on each side. Remove from the broiler and let rest for 10 minutes. Return to the oven and broil for 2 minutes, or until browned and a thermometer inserted in the center registers 145°F for medium-rare. Drizzle with the lemon juice and some of the chili oil and garnish with the mint. Season with additional sea salt and serve.

Oven-Roasted Lamb Shoulder

Lamb shoulder is a great cut of meat, too often overlooked in favor of more costly lamb chops and leg of lamb. When cooked properly, it is succulent and tender. Yes, it has saturated fat, but at 4 ounces of lamb per serving, it's not going to hurt and it will more than satisfy a meat craving. The spices and flavorings I use here are inspired by Portugal, where they use garlic, oregano, and piri piri peppers for a terrific chicken dish. Lemon-infused olive oil and fresh lemon juice cut through the fattiness for a sprightly flavor.

serves 6

1 lamb shoulder (2 pounds)

¼ cup lemon agrumato (lemon-infused olive oil)

15 cloves garlic, halved

1 cup fresh oregano leaves

20 piri piri chile peppers

Salt and fresh ground black pepper to taste

1 tablespoon paprika

Juice of 1 lemon

Preheat the oven to 325°F. Using a paring knife, make thirty 1-inch-deep, narrow slits all over the lamb. Rub the lamb all over with the lemon agrumato. Place the garlic, oregano, and piri piri chiles in the slits randomly. Rub the lamb liberally with the salt, black pepper, and paprika. Place the lamb in a roasting pan fitted with a rack. Roast until the lamb is crusty on the outside and a thermometer inserted in the center registers 160°F for medium, about 4 hours. Drizzle the lemon juice over the lamb. To serve, thinly slice the lamb across the grain. Serve with some good crusty bread and some onions and peppers.

Chorizo and Chickpeas with Charred Onions, Black Olives, and Herbs

Sausage, when used in smaller amounts, is a powerhouse flavor booster. If you get the really good Iberico chorizo from acorn-fed pigs, a lot of the fat is monounsaturated and polyunsaturated. You will find the combination of chorizo and chickpeas (representing the Christian and Muslim strains in Spanish cooking) to be a nice match, as I did in the old Moorish quarter of Sevilla. They served a cold chickpea salad with black olives and grilled chorizo that I thought, if accented with charred onions, would make a warming and hearty stew. Note that I say charred and not burnt. It's a fine line, but an important one.

serves 4

½ pound fresh chorizo

1 pound chickpeas, picked over and soaked overnight

2 medium onions, halved, divided

1 rib celery

2 cloves garlic

1 carrot

2 sprigs thyme

1 bay leaf

4 quarts water

1 teaspoon Spanish paprika

Salt and fresh ground black pepper to taste

1 cup pitted black olives

¼ cup fresh parsley leaves

¼ cup chopped fresh chives

¼ cup fresh cilantro leaves

¼ cup fresh chervil leaves

Juice of 2 lemons

3 tablespoons olive oil

Preheat a skillet over low heat for 5 minutes. Remove the chorizo from its casing and add it to the pan. Cook for 10 minutes, or until the chorizo has rendered out its excess fat. Set aside.

In a large pot, combine the chickpeas, half of the onions, the celery, garlic, carrot, thyme, and bay leaf. Fill with the water. Bring to a boil, then reduce the heat, cover, and simmer until the chickpeas are firm but tender, 45 to 50 minutes. Remove from the heat, add the rendered chorizo, the paprika, and the salt and pepper. Cover the pot and let sit for 25 minutes. Remove and discard the thyme and bay leaf.

Meanwhile, prepare a charcoal grill or preheat a gas grill. Grill the remaining onion until charred, about 5 minutes per side. When cool enough to handle, chop and fold the onion into the chickpeas. Add the olives, parsley, chives, cilantro, and chervil and gently stir to incorporate. Stir in the lemon juice and olive oil.

CHAPTER 6

COOKED VEGETABLES

Cooking often unlocks many of the nutrients locked inside the cells of a vegetable. Some vegetables, such as potatoes and yucca, are not even edible uncooked. Because heat breaks down foods into their flavor components, cooked vegetables as a rule are more complex and deeper in flavor. With cooked vegetables, as with everything else in this book, fat delivers and extends flavor. When vegetables are cooked in oil, the high heat often caramelizes the natural sugars found in all plants and yields a pleasing texture, golden crust, and sublime taste.

Cauliflower Couscous with Fresh Herbs, Currants, and Coconut 120

Curried Beets, Apple, Fried Shallots, and Walnuts 121

Charred Eggplant, Grilled Onions, Pickled Raisins, and Pine Nuts 122

Blistered Fairytale Eggplant Stewed in Olive Oil, Cherry Tomatoes, and Herbs 123

Peppers Stewed in Olive Oil, Herbs, and Garlic 124

Slow-Cooked Fennel in Olive Oil 125

Pan-Roasted Brussels Sprouts with Southeast Asian Flavors 128

Sautéed Broccoli with Garlic and Chiles 130

Blistered Broccoli with Garlic and Chiles 131

Grilled Portobello Mushroom Sandwiches with Arugula and Date-Walnut Pesto 134

Pan-Roasted Mushrooms, Herbs, and Spices | 135

Charred String Beans with Tofu-Miso Dressing | 137

Caramelized Sweet Potatoes with
Smoked Sea Salt and Pecorino | 138

Baked Sweet Potatoes, Granny Smith Apples,
Chives, and Walnuts | 140

Crisp-Baked Sweet Potatoes | 141

Portuguese Potatoes | 143

Spice-Dusted Potatoes | 144

Pumpkin Fries | 145

Acorn Squash, Hazelnuts, Parmesan,
and Acacia Honey | 146

Roasted Carrots with Sumac, Lemon, and Honey | 149

Roasted Carrots with Cumin and Avocado | 150

Cauliflower Couscous with Fresh Herbs, Currants, and Coconut

The famous French chef Alain Ducasse first turned me on to the idea of pulsing cauliflower in a food processor. When you do, it looks like couscous, but with far fewer carbs. It cooks very quickly, and the "grains" stay fluffy. I added a mix of Middle Eastern and Asian ingredients, and the result is something that the ancient Silk Road merchants might have eaten on their travels.

serves 4

3 cups cauliflower florets

1 cup boiling water

2 tablespoons canola oil or safflower oil

1 piece (2 inches) fresh ginger

1 tablespoon dry coconut flakes

1 tablespoon currants

1 tablespoon flesh cilantro, cut into ribbons

1 tablespoon fresh parsley, cut into ribbons

¼ teaspoon garam masala

¼ teaspoon cayenne pepper

Juice of 1 lemon

Salt to taste

Place the florets in the bowl of a food processor and pulse until the cauliflower begins to resemble couscous (taking care not to overpulse).

In a large skillet, combine the boiling water, oil, ginger, and cauliflower and simmer until fork-tender, about 4 minutes. Remove and discard the ginger.

Add the coconut, currants, cilantro, parsley, garam masala, cayenne pepper, and lemon juice and toss. Season with salt and serve alongside scallops, fish, or chicken.

Curried Beets, Apple, Fried Shallots, and Walnuts

Savory curry pairs well with sweet vegetables such as beets or onions. Here we impart the flavor of curry in a very interesting and simple way. I boil the beets in curry water instead of the traditional vinegar water, allowing the beets to pick up curry flavor. I save vinegar for the dressing so that it comes through as a bright accent.

serves 4

1 pound golden beets

1 tablespoon Madras curry powder

1 tablespoon salt

for the vinaigrette:

6 tablespoons canola oil

3 tablespoons white balsamic vinegar

1 tablespoon Dijon mustard

Salt and fresh ground black pepper to taste

for the fried shallots:

2 large shallots, peeled and sliced in thin rings

2 tablespoons amaranth flour

3 tablespoons extra virgin olive oil

for the salad:

1 Granny Smith apple, peel on, cored and diced

1 cup walnut pieces, toasted

1 teaspoon chopped cilantro

1 teaspoon chopped fresh parsley

¼ cup fried shallots

Salt and fresh ground black pepper to taste

In a 4-quart pot, combine the beets, curry powder, and salt. Fill with water to cover. Bring to a boil. Reduce the heat and simmer until the beets are fork-tender, 30 to 50 minutes. Turn off the heat and let the beets cool in the liquid.

to make the vinaigrette:

Meanwhile, in a medium bowl, whisk together the canola oil, vinegar, mustard, and salt and pepper. Set aside. When the beets are cool enough to handle, peel and quarter them. Add the beets to the vinaigrette, toss, and marinate, covered, overnight.

to make the fried shallots:

Place the shallots in a large bowl and sprinkle them with the amaranth flour. Then put the dusted shallots in a sieve and shake off any excess flour.

In a deep frying pan over medium heat, heat the oil until rippling, then fry the shallots in batches until golden. Drain on a paper towel–covered plate.

to make the salad:

In a large bowl, combine the beets, apple, walnuts, cilantro, parsley, and shallots. Toss to coat. Season with salt and pepper and serve.

Charred Eggplant, Grilled Onions, Pickled Raisins, and Pine Nuts

This is my deconstructed and reconstructed take on one of the jewels of the Sicilian kitchen—caponata. I want eggplant to be the star here. Normally when you combine eggplant with such highly flavored ingredients as grilled onion and pickled raisins, it tends to recede into the background. You know you're eating something smooth and mushy, but it has no character. This runs counter to my whole philosophy; if you can't taste it, then you don't need it. Magic happens when you char the eggplant; the flavor and smokiness really pop, and it becomes the star of the dish. Grilling the onion gives you char and sweetness to match up with the eggplant, and pickling the raisins softens them and creates little explosions of sweet flavor.

serves 4

for the pickled raisins:

- ¼ cup raisins
- 2 tablespoons red wine vinegar
- ¼ cup water
- 1 tablespoon salt
- 1 tablespoon sugar

for the eggplant and onions:

- 1½ pounds eggplant, left whole
- 9 tablespoons extra virgin olive oil, divided
- Salt and fresh ground black pepper to taste
- 1 Vidalia onion, cut into ½-inch-thick slices
- 3 tablespoons pine nuts, toasted
- 1 tablespoon chopped fresh parsley leaves
- Juice of 1 lemon
- Zest of ½ lemon
- 2 tablespoons balsamic vinegar
- Sea salt to taste

to make the pickled raisins:

In a 1-quart stainless steel saucepan, combine the raisins, red wine vinegar, water, salt, and sugar. Bring to a boil. Remove from the heat and let sit for 30 minutes.

to make the eggplant and onions:

Prepare a charcoal grill or preheat a gas grill. Alternatively, preheat the broiler. Rub the eggplants all over with 3 tablespoons of the olive oil and season with salt and pepper. Place the onion slices on a sheet of foil and toss with 5 tablespoons of the olive oil. Season with salt and pepper. Grill or broil the eggplants, turning multiple times, until they are charred all over and fork-tender, about 15 minutes. At the same time, grill or broil the onion slices until blistered and tender, turning once.

Using a sharp knife, gently cut the eggplants in half lengthwise and then into bite-size pieces. Add the pickled raisins, onion slices, pine nuts, parsley, lemon juice, and lemon zest. Drizzle with the balsamic vinegar, the remaining 1 tablespoon olive oil, and sea salt. Serve with pitas or spooned over grilled chicken or fish.

Blistered Fairytale Eggplant Stewed in Olive Oil, Cherry Tomatoes, and Herbs

These little treasures are found in the greenmarket in summertime for a few short weeks. Get them while you can. They are small, beautiful, and have a wonderfully delicate flavor. The skin is very tender and the flesh cooks quickly, plus they're not in the least bit bitter (as other, often larger eggplants tend to be). Chances are, when you find these pretty babies, you will often come across sweet cherry tomatoes.

serves 4

¼ cup extra virgin olive oil

2 teaspoons red-pepper flakes

1 shallot, thinly sliced

3 cloves garlic

1 pound fairytale eggplants

Sea salt and fresh ground black pepper to taste

1 pint cherry tomatoes

1 tablespoon sherry vinegar

2 sprigs thyme

1 bay leaf

1 tablespoon fresh parsley leaves

1 teaspoon chopped fresh basil

1 teaspoon chopped fresh mint

Zest and juice of ½ lemon

In a large skillet over medium-high heat, warm the oil. Add the pepper flakes, shallot, garlic, and fairytale eggplants and season with sea salt and black pepper. Cook, stirring frequently, until the eggplants begin to blister. Add the tomatoes and toss together with the eggplants. Add the vinegar, thyme, and bay leaf and, using a wooden spoon, scrape up any bits that have stuck to the bottom of the pan. Reduce the heat to low, cover, and cook for 5 minutes. The tomatoes will break down to create a sauce. Add the parsley, basil, mint, lemon zest, and lemon juice and stir gently to incorporate. Remove and discard the thyme and bay leaf. Serve in a big bowl with lots of crusty bread or ladle over pasta.

Peppers Stewed in Olive Oil, Herbs, and Garlic

This is one of my go-to side dishes. Side with what, you ask? Pretty much everything: fish, chicken, lamb, a crusty steak, a bowl of quinoa. Puree it and it makes a sweet herbaceous condiment. Served with a piece of hard cheese, like manchego, and some crusty bread, it's a nice light supper, made even nicer with a light white wine . . . say, an Albarino.

serves 4

---

1 cup olive oil

1½ pounds red bell peppers, halved and seeded

1 onion, cut in half and thinly sliced

4 cloves garlic, sliced

1 sprig thyme

1 sprig oregano

1 bay leaf

Zest and juice of ½ lemon

2 tablespoons white wine

Salt and fresh ground black pepper to taste

In a 2-quart saucepan, combine the olive oil, bell peppers, onion, garlic, thyme, oregano, bay leaf, lemon zest, lemon juice, and white wine and bring to a boil. Reduce the heat and simmer until the onion and peppers soften, about 45 minutes. Remove from the heat and allow to cool. Remove and discard the thyme and bay leaf. Season to taste with the salt and black pepper. Serve on its own with some grilled bread or use it with chicken, pork, fish, or whatever you like.

Slow-Cooked Fennel in Olive Oil

Fennel is like that actor in a movie whom you don't notice at first, but then, as you get deeper into the film, you discover that he or she is the real scene stealer. There are so many things that fennel goes with and so many things a cook can do with it. Braise it and pair it with fish or chicken. Char it on the grill. Add it to risotto. Cook it in any stock and it will pick up flavors like a sponge. Bouillabaisse isn't really bouilla-baisse without it. When you slow cook, as I call for here, you can then use the olive oil in a salad dressing or a pasta sauce.

serves 4

1 cup olive oil

½ cup white wine

½ cup water

4 cloves garlic

2 shallots

2 sprigs thyme

1 bay leaf

2 pounds fennel, tough outer layers trimmed, split in half, ends left intact

In a large pan, combine the olive oil, wine, water, garlic, shallots, thyme, bay leaf, and fennel. Bring to a boil over high heat. Reduce the heat and simmer until the fennel is soft and tender, about 30 to 45 minutes. Let cool in its liquid. Remove the thyme and bay leaf. Serve whole or cut into small wedges. Alternately, after slow cooking, caramelize the fennel by removing the liquid in the pan and browning the fennel on medium heat for 10 minutes on each side.

Slow-Cooked Fennel
in Olive Oil

Pan-Roasted Brussels Sprouts with Southeast Asian Flavors

I think of Brussels sprouts as the Little League versions of cabbage. Well, at least they are small like Little Leaguers, but a bit more manageable than a team of 8-year-olds. On second thought, make that *a lot* more manageable than a team of 8-year-olds. Anyway, Brussels sprouts are also tender, with a slight mustardy bite. They caramelize beautifully, developing sweetness. Though they are little critters, they have the gutsiness to stand up to a medley of Southeast Asian flavors.

serves 4

2 tablespoons coconut oil

1 pound Brussels sprouts, outer leaves and root ends trimmed, cut in half

1 tablespoon gluten-free tamari

1 teaspoon sugar

1 teaspoon Madras curry powder

1 teaspoon ground ginger

1 teaspoon garlic powder

1 teaspoon chopped scallions

1 teaspoon chopped Thai red chile pepper (wear plastic gloves when handling)

1 teaspoon sesame seeds

Zest and juice of ½ lemon

Salt and fresh ground black pepper to taste

1 teaspoon dry coconut flakes

1 teaspoon fresh chopped cilantro

In a skillet or wok over high heat, warm the coconut oil. Add the Brussels sprouts and cook until golden brown, about 6 minutes. Add the tamari, sugar, curry powder, ginger, garlic powder, scallions, red chile pepper, and sesame seeds and toss. Transfer to a serving bowl, add the lemon zest and juice, and season with the salt and black pepper. Garnish with the coconut and cilantro and serve.

Sautéed Broccoli with Garlic and Chiles

For all those picky eaters who never liked broccoli, here is the method that seals the deal and turns them into broccoli lovers—or at least broccoli likers. I use the dressing that Italians pour on their broccoli rabe, which is a leafy relative of regular broccoli. Deglazing the pan with water after you have sautéed the vegetables in oil creates a super-steamy eruption that finishes the broccoli through and through. Neat trick! When the water evaporates, it draws sugars out of the broccoli, creating a caramelized finish.

serves 4

¼ cup extra virgin olive oil

3 cloves garlic, thinly sliced

1 teaspoon red-pepper flakes or 1 red jalapeño chile pepper, thinly sliced (wear plastic gloves when handling)

1 pound broccoli, cut into small florets

2 tablespoons water

1 teaspoon red wine vinegar

Salt and fresh ground black pepper to taste

In a medium skillet over medium-high heat, warm the olive oil. Add the garlic and pepper flakes or jalapeño pepper and cook until fragrant, 1 minute. Add the broccoli and cook, stirring frequently, until it turns bright green and starts to brown, about 3 minutes. Add the water to the pan and cook for 3 minutes, or until the water evaporates. Remove from the heat. Drizzle with the vinegar, season with salt and black pepper, and serve.

Blistered Broccoli with Garlic and Chiles

This is a variation on the preceding recipe, but charring makes all the difference. This method of almost-but-not-quite burning has been popularized by Francis Mallmann, the great Argentine chef. He finds that in the fine line just before things burn, the flavor deepens as the sugars caramelize. You are not charring the whole broccoli, just the outside, so you still have the fresh, juicy flavor of a green vegetable for contrast. This method also works with arugula, lettuces, and chard. Play around with it!

serves 4

1 head broccoli, cut into 16 pieces

¼ cup extra virgin olive oil

2 cloves garlic, thinly sliced

1 teaspoon red-pepper flakes

Juice and zest of 1 lemon

Sea salt to taste

Preheat a cast-iron griddle over high heat. Place the broccoli on the dry griddle and char until blistered on one side. Turn and char the other side. Transfer to a large heatproof bowl.

In a large skillet over medium heat, warm the olive oil. Add the garlic and pepper flakes and cook, stirring frequently, until the garlic is golden brown, about 2 minutes. Pour the oil over the broccoli and turn to coat. Allow to marinate for 10 minutes. Drizzle with the lemon juice, season with the sea salt and lemon zest, and serve hot or at room temperature.

Blistered Broccoli
with Garlic and Chiles

Grilled Portobello Mushroom Sandwiches with Arugula and Date-Walnut Pesto

I was inspired to create this by a serving of Kobe beef and dates at Alinea in Chicago. Somehow my synapses made the leap to portobello mushrooms and dates. I guess this goes to show you how a good meal and a couple of glasses of wine can unleash your inner chef. The key to portobellos is to grill them dry. Also, they are so full of liquid that you want to save your marinating for afterward—unless you like really soggy mushrooms. When I take them off the grill, they are still hot and weep liquid, enriching the marinade. The date-walnut pesto is sweet, savory, and tart—almost like a chutney for the meaty mushrooms.

serves 4

---

2 tablespoons extra virgin olive oil

1 tablespoon red wine vinegar

1 teaspoon white balsamic vinegar or lemon juice

Leaves from 2 sprigs thyme

1 clove garlic

1 teaspoon sea salt

1 teaspoon fresh ground black pepper

4 portobello mushrooms, stems trimmed and gills removed with a spoon

4 cups arugula

for the pesto:

⅓ cup chopped dates

⅓ cup walnuts, toasted and chopped

2 tablespoons extra virgin olive oil

2 tablespoons finely grated Parmesan cheese

2 tablespoons chopped fresh parsley

Salt and fresh ground black pepper to taste

4 small ciabatta rolls, split open and toasted

In a large shallow dish, whisk together the olive oil, red wine vinegar, balsamic vinegar or lemon juice, thyme, garlic, sea salt, and pepper to make a marinade.

Prepare a charcoal grill or preheat a gas grill. Alternatively, preheat a grill pan. Grill the mushrooms until they begin to exude liquid and soften, about 5 minutes. Toss the mushrooms with the marinade and cover to allow the mushrooms to steam in their own heat, 15 minutes.

to make the pesto:

In a food processor, combine the dates, walnuts, olive oil, cheese, and parsley. Pulse to barely combine. Season with the salt and pepper and set aside.

Remove the mushrooms from the marinade and set the marinade aside. Cut the mushrooms into 2-inch-thick slices. In a medium bowl, toss the arugula with the reserved marinade, using it as a vinaigrette to dress the arugula.

To make the sandwiches, spread both sides of the ciabatta rolls with the pesto. Arrange the mushrooms on one half of each roll, top with the arugula, and cover with the other half of the roll.

Pan-Roasted Mushrooms, Herbs, and Spices

In Spain, roasted mushrooms with a light dressing are a standby at tapas bars. Come to think of it, when you say the word "bar" in Spain, you can pretty much assume that tapas are part of the deal. This simple recipe is most often made with cremini mushrooms, which are also known as button mushrooms. They are the most common 'shrooms in most markets—both here and in Spain. But in recent years as farmers' markets have sprung up all across America, the variety of mushrooms has . . . pardon the expression . . . mushroomed. These days, many supermarkets have also hopped on the 'shroom bandwagon, and I have become fond of cooking this dish with a variety of them. The different tastes and textures are lovely. Oyster mushrooms are a new fave because of the way the ends get crisper and caramelize and the ribs are slithery and tender. I've tried chanterelles, trumpets, and hen-of-the-woods, too. The only mushroom I have found that is a little too aggressive for this recipe is the shiitake. But, hey, maybe that's just me.

serves 4

3 tablespoons extra virgin olive oil, divided

8 ounces cremini mushrooms, cleaned and trimmed, quartered

2 sprigs thyme, divided

3 cloves garlic, halved, divided

½ teaspoon red-pepper flakes, divided

Salt and fresh ground black pepper to taste

8 ounces oyster mushrooms, cleaned and trimmed, separated

1 tablespoon chopped fresh parsley

Juice of ½ lemon

In a large skillet over medium heat, warm 1 tablespoon of the olive oil. Add the cremini mushrooms, 1 sprig of thyme, half of the garlic, and ¼ teaspoon of the pepper flakes. Season with salt and black pepper and cook, stirring frequently, until fragrant and the mushrooms release their juices, about 8 minutes. Using a slotted spoon, transfer the mushrooms to a plate. Repeat with the oyster mushrooms, 1 tablespoon of the olive oil, and the remaining thyme, garlic, and pepper flakes. Add the cremini mushrooms back to the pan, toss, and sprinkle with the parsley. Season to taste with additional salt and black pepper and drizzle with the remaining 1 tablespoon olive oil.

Charred String Beans with Tofu-Miso Dressing

This recipe is my take on sumiso, one of the fundamental dressings or condiments of Japanese cuisine. The traditional version is made with a mixture of miso, egg yolks, mirin, and sugar that is cooked down until it becomes as thick as mayonnaise. Instead of using eggs, I went vegan with tofu and eliminated the cooking step for sumiso. I think you get much more flavor this way. If you are a glutton for even more flavor, add ginger, garlic, and scallions to supercharge this recipe. I find these ingredients balance the char on the string beans and complement the "green" flavor of the uncharred parts.

serves 4

1 pound string beans, tops and tails trimmed

2 tablespoons extra virgin olive oil

Salt and fresh ground black pepper to taste

for the dressing:

¼ cup white miso

¼ cup soft tofu

1 tablespoon Dijon mustard

2 tablespoons aji-mirin

1 tablespoon rice wine vinegar

2 tablespoons grapeseed oil

Salt and fresh ground black pepper to taste

for the garnish:

1 tablespoon toasted sesame seeds

¼ cup diced firm tofu

Heat a cast-iron skillet over high heat for 5 minutes. Add the beans and char until blistered on both sides, turning once, about 2 minutes per side. Transfer to a serving bowl. Drizzle the olive oil over the beans and toss. Season with salt and pepper. Set aside.

to make the dressing:

In a food processor, combine the miso, tofu, mustard, aji-mirin, vinegar, and grapeseed oil. Pulse until smooth. Season with the salt and pepper. Pour the dressing over the beans. Garnish with the sesame seeds and diced tofu and serve.

Caramelized Sweet Potatoes with Smoked Sea Salt and Pecorino

I get an earthy, sweet, and nicely crusted effect by baking the sweet potatoes twice. This simple technique caramelizes the natural sugars. Smoked sea salt infuses the sweet potatoes with grilled flavor without grilling. Finish with Pecorino and you have big flavor that goes nicely with barbecue. Obviously, vegans will want to skip the cheese. But with or without, make sure you eat the whole potato, skin and all.

serves 4

2 sweet potatoes (about ½ pound each)

1 tablespoon canola oil

1 teaspoon smoked sea salt

1 teaspoon sea salt

½ teaspoon fresh cracked black pepper

¼ teaspoon cayenne pepper

1 teaspoon fresh lemon juice

2 tablespoons grated Pecorino cheese (optional)

Preheat the oven to 350°F. Coat the sweet potatoes with the oil and place on a parchment-lined baking sheet. Bake until fork-tender, about 35 minutes. Set aside to cool. Increase the heat to 500°F. Slice the potatoes in half and return to the baking sheet flesh side up. Bake until the potatoes are blistered and begin to char, 10 to 12 minutes. Transfer the potatoes to a serving platter. Meanwhile, in a small bowl, combine the smoked sea salt, sea salt, black pepper, and cayenne pepper. Season the potatoes with the salt mixture. Drizzle the lemon juice over and garnish with the cheese, if using.

Baked Sweet Potatoes, Granny Smith Apples, Chives, and Walnuts

For many people, sweet potatoes are something you eat at Thanksgiving either candied or with marshmallows. I came up with this recipe for *People* magazine and received a lot of requests for it, along with follow-up questions and suggestions. Either this shows the power of the press or the power of the sweet potato. Everybody always asks for seconds.

serves 4

1½ pounds sweet potatoes (about 3)

1 teaspoon butter

¼ cup walnut halves, toasted

1 teaspoon brown sugar

¼ teaspoon cayenne pepper

Salt and fresh ground black pepper to taste

2 Granny Smith apples

1 teaspoon fresh lemon juice

1 tablespoon chopped chives

1 tablespoon extra virgin olive oil

Preheat the oven to 350°F. Place the whole sweet potatoes on a piece of foil and roast until the flesh is tender and the skin is crisp, 35 to 45 minutes.

Meanwhile, in a medium skillet, melt the butter. Add the walnuts, brown sugar, cayenne pepper, and salt and black pepper. Reduce the heat to medium low and cook, stirring frequently, until the sugar begins to bubble and froth up, turning golden brown and coating the nuts. Carefully transfer the nuts to a nonstick surface. (Be careful not to touch the nuts until they are cooled.) Break the nuts into chunks and set aside. Dice the apples and place them in a medium bowl. Add the lemon juice and salt and black pepper to taste. Toss to combine. Add the reserved walnuts and the chives and toss.

Cut the sweet potatoes in half lengthwise. Top with the apple mixture, drizzle with the olive oil, and serve.

Crisp-Baked Sweet Potatoes

Just as in the previous recipe, I bake these instead of frying them, so there is much less fat involved. In the last minutes of baking, the addition of maple syrup helps crisp things nicely. I find them highly addictive, but then what else would you expect from something that is sweet, salty, and crisp?

serves 4

3 large sweet potatoes, scrubbed, peeled, and cut into ¼-inch-thick matchsticks

¼ cup canola oil

Sea salt and fresh ground black pepper to taste

2 tablespoons maple syrup

Combine the sweet potatoes and canola oil in a bowl and toss to coat. Season with the salt and pepper and let sit for at least 1 hour or up to 4 hours. Preheat the oven to 350°F. Spread the sweet potatoes in a single layer on a sheet pan and roast for 5 minutes. Remove and let cool. Drizzle the maple syrup over, toss to coat, and bake for 4 minutes. Serve immediately.

Portuguese Potatoes

I ate these unforgettable potatoes along with a perfect rotisserie chicken on a warm summer night when my girlfriend and I literally followed our noses to a restaurant in the Portuguese seaside town of Cascais. The aroma was irresistible. As with so much wonderful food in Portugal, it was supremely simple. I particularly like using shallots, which, when roasted, develop a flavor that pulls savoriness out of anything you eat them with.

serves 4

4 large Idaho potatoes, washed, dried, and cut into 1-inch chunks

5 cloves garlic, chopped

2 shallots, chopped

2 tablespoons paprika

¼ cup olive oil

Sea salt and fresh ground black pepper to taste

¼ cup chopped parsley

Juice of 1 lemon

Preheat the oven to 350°F. In a large bowl, combine the potatoes, garlic, shallots, paprika, olive oil, and sea salt and pepper. Toss to evenly coat. Spread the potatoes in a single layer on a baking sheet. Roast until tender and crisp, about 25 minutes. Transfer to a bowl and toss with the parsley and lemon juice.

Spice-Dusted Potatoes

I don't call these crispy potatoes french fries because they're not French and they're not fried. They get their golden crust from baking in just a little bit of healthy canola oil. So far as the spicing goes, most folks think this combo is a home run, but feel free to experiment.

serves 4

4 medium Idaho potatoes, unpeeled

½ cup canola oil or olive oil, divided

1 teaspoon garlic powder

½ teaspoon cayenne pepper

½ teaspoon paprika

½ teaspoon ground cumin

½ teaspoon onion powder

½ teaspoon fresh ground black pepper

1-2 tablespoons kosher salt, as needed

Preheat the oven (preferably set on convection) to 350°F. Have ready a large bowl of cold water. Cut the potatoes into 1-inch strips as for french fries. Put them in the water as you go. Drain the fries and toss them in a bowl with ¼ cup of the oil. Arrange the potatoes on a baking sheet in a single layer and bake until wilted, about 10 minutes. Remove from the oven and let cool.

Increase the oven temperature to 500°F. Toss the fries in the remaining ¼ cup oil, return to the baking sheet, and bake until golden brown and crispy, about 10 minutes. Meanwhile, in a small bowl, combine the garlic powder, cayenne pepper, paprika, cumin, onion powder, black pepper, and salt. Transfer the fries to a platter and season to taste with the spice mixture.

Pumpkin Fries

Yes, there is life for pumpkins beyond pumpkin pie. Although, now that I think about it, I adore pumpkin pie and feel it's a tragedy that most of us eat it only once a year. So, for these baked fries, I combine some of the signature flavors of the holiday staple with onion and garlic powder. The result is a familiar and beloved flavor with a savory accent.

serves 4

1 sugar pumpkin (1½ pounds), cut into ¼-inch-thick fries

½ cup canola oil, divided

½ teaspoon maple sugar

1 teaspoon garlic powder

½ teaspoon cayenne pepper

½ teaspoon fresh ground black pepper

½ teaspoon onion powder

¼ teaspoon ground cinnamon

1–2 tablespoons kosher salt, as needed

Preheat the oven (preferably set on convection) to 350°F. In a large bowl, toss the fries with ¼ cup of the canola oil. Spread on a baking sheet in a single layer and bake for 15 minutes. Remove from the oven and let cool. Increase the oven temperature to 500°F. Drizzle the remaining ¼ cup canola oil on the fries and toss to coat. Bake until golden brown and crispy, about 5 minutes. Meanwhile, in a small bowl, combine the maple sugar, garlic powder, cayenne pepper, black pepper, onion powder, cinnamon, and kosher salt. Transfer the potatoes to a bowl and season with the spice mixture to taste. Return the potatoes to the baking sheet and bake for 5 minutes. Let cool before serving.

Acorn Squash, Hazelnuts, Parmesan, and Acacia Honey

Sometimes people confuse great cooking with how many ingredients you can include in a recipe. This is not the way I look at things at all. I never want to do so much that the flavor or character of the main ingredient is lost. Acorn squash is such a forceful presence that you can throw a lot at it and it still shines through. Here I use it as a base that happily accepts Parmesan cheese, honey, lemon juice, and fiery cayenne. The end result is hearty enough to be a one-dish meal, and distinct enough to accompany a Sunday roast chicken, or a pan-roasted pork chop.

serves 4

1 acorn squash, seeded and cut into 8 wedges

1 tablespoon sea salt

½ teaspoon cayenne pepper

1 tablespoon extra virgin olive oil

2 tablespoons acacia honey

2 tablespoons grated Parmesan cheese

¼ cup blanched hazelnuts, toasted

1 tablespoon parsley leaves

Juice of 1 lemon

Preheat the oven to 350°F. In a baking dish, place the acorn squash flesh side up. Season with the sea salt and cayenne pepper and then drizzle with the olive oil. Cover with foil. Bake until fork-tender, about 35 minutes. Remove the foil and drizzle the squash with the honey. Bake for 5 minutes. Arrange on a platter and sprinkle with the cheese. Garnish with the hazelnuts and parsley, and drizzle the lemon juice over. Serve warm.

Roasted Carrots with Sumac, Lemon, and Honey

Compare this recipe with the one on page 150. Isn't it wonderful how a carrot can change personalities with just a few different ingredients? This variation of roasted carrots relies on Middle Eastern flavors. Sumac contributes the tartness of a puckery lemon without adding liquid. The multi-herb dressing recalls midsummer freshness even in the dead of winter.

serves 4

for the carrots:

- 1 pound tricolor carrots, scrubbed
- ¼ cup olive oil
- 2 tablespoons fresh lemon juice
- 3 cloves garlic, minced
- 2 sprigs thyme
- Salt and fresh ground black pepper to taste
- 2 tablespoons honey

for the dressing:

- 1 teaspoon chopped dill
- 1 teaspoon chopped fresh parsley
- 1 teaspoon chopped cilantro
- 1 teaspoon ground sumac
- 1 teaspoon lemon juice
- 1 teaspoon olive oil

to make the carrots:

Preheat the oven to 450°F. In a bowl, combine the carrots with the olive oil, lemon juice, garlic, thyme, and salt and pepper. Arrange in a single layer in a roasting pan and roast for 25 minutes. Drizzle the honey over the carrots, toss to coat, and roast for 5 minutes. Remove and discard the thyme.

to make the dressing:

Meanwhile, in a small bowl, combine the dill, parsley, cilantro, sumac, lemon juice, and olive oil.

Transfer the carrots to a serving bowl, pour the herb dressing over, and toss. Serve warm or chilled.

Roasted Carrots with Cumin and Avocado

This salad was inspired by a trip to my friend Dan Kluger's restaurant, ABC Kitchen. I added the flavors of cumin and then gave it another southwestern boost with jalapeño. From my grandma, I borrowed the trick of adding honey. This is a great side for pork chops or lamb. Or serve it with a simply prepared quinoa. Puree it with avocado and you've got carrot guacamole. Sounds weird, tastes great.

serves 4

for the carrots:

- 2 tablespoons sherry vinegar
- ¼ cup olive oil
- 1 tablespoon cumin seeds, toasted
- 3 cloves garlic, minced
- 2 sprigs thyme
- 1 pound tricolor carrots, scrubbed
- Salt and fresh ground black pepper to taste
- 2 avocados, cut into ½-inch cubes

for the vinaigrette:

- ¼ cup olive oil
- 2 tablespoons lemon juice
- 1 tablespoon honey
- 1 clove garlic, minced
- 1 teaspoon cumin seeds, toasted
- ½ jalapeño chile pepper, seeded and minced (wear plastic gloves when handling)
- 2 tablespoons chopped cilantro
- Salt and fresh ground black pepper to taste

to make the carrots:

Preheat the oven to 450°F. In a large bowl, whisk together the vinegar, olive oil, cumin seeds, garlic, and thyme. Add the carrots, toss, and season with salt and black pepper. Arrange in a single layer on a baking sheet and roast until the carrots are tender, about 20 minutes. Remove and discard the thyme.

to make the vinaigrette:

Meanwhile, in a small bowl, whisk together the olive oil, lemon juice, honey, garlic, cumin seeds, jalapeño pepper, and cilantro. Season with the salt and black pepper.

Transfer the carrots to a serving bowl. Pour the vinaigrette over and toss to coat. Fold in the avocado and serve.

CHAPTER 7

DESSERTS

I'll admit it: Desserts are a test for healthy eating. They are usually a perfect storm of calories as sugar, flour, fat, and some salt combine to produce the recipes highest in calories and fat. Often I will choose a healthier no-fuss dessert of fresh fruit in season when its flavor is fully developed and hard to beat for deliciousness. But there are times when something sweet and creamy is what you want, and you're not to be denied. In this short chapter, I show you a few of the ways I have handled the dessert challenge. Some of them are gluten and lactose free, and most are completely free of refined sugar. Plus, the fats come from nuts, avocados, and olive oil. Once you get the hang of how I handled these ingredients, I am sure you will come up with your own sweet inventions.

Cashew Panna Cotta with Tropical Fruit | 154

Baked Apples with Walnuts and Raisins | 156

Banana and Almond Freeze | 157

Date and Walnut Cookies | 158

Maria's Ravani | 159

Avocado Ice Cream with Lime and Coconut | 161

Cashew Panna Cotta with Tropical Fruit

Panna cotta is a lovely custardlike Italian dessert made with heavy cream. Instead, I use cashew milk with gelatin. Cashews come from the tropics, so acting on the theory of food combinations that says "if it grows together, it goes together," I decided to add tropical fruits. Finally, for reasons only known to my subconscious, I thought cilantro would do something nice by way of tying it all together.

serves 4

2 cups cashew milk, divided

4½ teaspoons gelatin powder

½ cup coconut sugar

3 cardamom pods

½ vanilla bean, split and seeds scraped away

⅓ cup chopped pineapple

⅓ cup chopped mango

⅓ cup chopped papaya

2 tablespoons lime juice

2 tablespoons cashew pieces, toasted

3 sprigs mint, leaves picked and cut into thin ribbons

2 sprigs cilantro, leaves picked and cut into thin ribbons

In a mixing bowl, combine ⅓ cup of the cashew milk and the gelatin. Stir and set aside.

In a 2-quart saucepan, combine the coconut sugar, the remaining 1⅔ cups cashew milk, the cardamom pods, and vanilla bean and bring to a boil. Add the gelatin mixture to the hot cashew milk and stir for 1 minute over high heat. Remove the cardamom pods and vanilla bean and pour the mixture into 4 ramekins. Chill in the refrigerator overnight.

In a medium bowl, combine the pineapple, mango, papaya, and lime juice and allow the mixture to macerate for at least 1 hour. Invert each panna cotta onto a dessert plate and spoon the fruit over the top. Garnish with the cashews, mint, and cilantro.

Baked Apples with Walnuts and Raisins

Basically, this is nothing more than an apple pie without the pie crust and with heart-healthy walnuts. No crust means it's gluten free and lower in fat, but just as comforting, especially when you serve it warm.

serves 4

½ cup walnuts, toasted and coarsely chopped

¼ cup golden raisins, soaked in water for 1 hour

Juice of 1 lemon

¼ cup maple syrup

4 small Cortland or McIntosh apples, peels on, tops cut off and cores removed

¼ cup water

1 tablespoon butter, divided

Preheat the oven to 350°F. In a medium bowl, combine the walnuts, raisins, lemon juice, and maple syrup. Arrange the apples, cored end up, in a baking dish and pour the water into the bottom. Spoon the nut mixture into each apple. Top each with a quarter of the butter. Cover the dish with foil and bake until the apples are soft but still hold their shape, about 25 minutes. Let cool and top with ice cream.

Banana and Almond Freeze

Bananas are so sweet and rich. When pureed, they are as creamy as traditional ice cream. Once again, heart-healthy almond milk makes for a smooth treat, but the fat is overwhelmingly of the healthy kind.

serves 4

3 cups sliced (1-inch thick) frozen overripe bananas

¼ cup agave syrup or maple syrup

¼ cup almond milk

¼ cup almonds

½ teaspoon ground cinnamon

¼ teaspoon vanilla extract

In a blender, combine the bananas, agave or maple syrup, almond milk, almonds, cinnamon, and vanilla. Blend until smooth. Serve immediately. The mixture can be frozen and scooped, but it's always best right out of the blender.

Date and Walnut Cookies

I came up with this recipe for my son when he was on a raw diet. In contrast to many desserts that are loaded with saturated fats and refined sugar, the fat from the nuts is very heart healthy and there is zero refined sugar. The lemon juice soak balances the sweetness of the dates, and it also brings out more of the nut flavor. Why? I am not sure, but I tried this a number of ways, and this combination of flavor and texture works, which is answer enough for me. It's very crumbly, more like halvah than a crunchy cookie.

serves 4

1 cup almond flour

1 cup chopped walnuts, divided

15 dates, pitted and soaked in lemon juice for $\frac{1}{2}$ hour, then drained

$\frac{1}{4}$ teaspoon sea salt

1 tablespoon ground cinnamon

In a food processor, combine the almond flour, $\frac{1}{2}$ cup of the walnuts, the dates, and the salt. Process until the mixture forms a dough. Add the remaining $\frac{1}{2}$ cup walnuts and pulse for 30 seconds just to incorporate.

Turn out the dough onto a clean work surface and roll into a 2-inch-thick cylinder using plastic wrap. Chill in the refrigerator overnight.

Slice the dough into $\frac{1}{2}$-inch-thick disks and sprinkle the cinnamon on top. Serve as is or, for a more cookielike consistency, place in a dehydrator set to 105°F and bake for 5 hours or bake in the oven on the lowest setting for 45 minutes. Let cool before eating.

Maria's Ravani

Ravani is a traditional Mediterranean diet cake made with almonds and semolina flour. I owe this version to Maria Loi, a gifted chef whose restaurant, Loi, is one of the best healthy eating places in New York. By best, I mean that the food is great and the ingredients healthy. The fat in this recipe comes entirely from olive oil and almonds. Semolina flour has gluten, so it's not a gluten-free dessert. This serves 8 people, so don't be surprised by the amount of sugar called for.

serves 8

1¾ cups granulated sugar

3 cups water

1 cup + 1 tablespoon olive oil

Zest of ½ orange

Zest of ½ tangerine

9 ounces fine semolina flour

8.5 ounces coarse semolina flour

½ cup whole blanched almonds, skinned

Confectioners' sugar, for garnish

In a large saucepan over medium heat, combine the sugar, water, 1 cup of the olive oil, and the orange and tangerine zest. Cook until the mixture comes to a boil. Reduce the heat to a simmer and use a wooden spoon to stir in the fine and coarse semolina. Stir continuously until the mixture thickens and peels away from the sides of the pan. Remove the saucepan from the heat and allow the mixture to cool for 5 minutes.

Meanwhile, preheat the oven to 350°F. Using a pastry brush, lightly coat a rimmed baking sheet with the remaining 1 tablespoon olive oil. Gently press the semolina mixture into the baking sheet, using a silicone spatula or your hands and pushing it out to the edges. Using a paring knife, score the semolina into 1-inch squares. Press an almond into the center of each square.

Bake until the surface is light golden brown, 40 to 50 minutes. Let cool completely. Tap the confectioners' sugar through a sieve over the cake for decoration.

Avocado Ice Cream with Lime and Coconut

The texture of the avocado ice cream is creamy, almost like a gelato. I think that is because its healthy fat content is so high, it behaves just like ice cream when it comes out of the freezer—but it has no dairy and no eggs. This can also be a nice appetizer if you fold in fresh tomatoes—a sweet guacamole. Hemp milk, available in many health food stores, is very digestible and contains a healthy balance of omega-6s and omega-3s.

serves 4

4 large avocados

Juice and zest of 1 lime

2 cups unsweetened hemp milk or rice milk

¾ cup coconut sugar

½ teaspoon sea salt

¼ cup coconut milk

2 tablespoons dry coconut flakes

Pit and peel the avocados. In a blender, combine the avocados, lime juice, hemp or rice milk, coconut sugar, and salt. Puree. Transfer the mixture to a medium mixing bowl, add the coconut milk, and whisk to combine.

Chill in the refrigerator for 3 to 4 hours to allow the mixture to cool down and the flavors to meld together. Place in an ice cream machine and process according to the manufacturer's directions. Check the mixture at 5 to 6 minutes to see if it is set. (Because of the viscosity of the mixture, this will set much faster than a normal anglaise.) Scoop into bowls and garnish with the coconut flakes and lime zest.

CHAPTER 8

NIBBLES AND NOSHES

When you are hanging out before a meal having cocktails or some wine, or spending a few hours watching TV, it's nice to have something to munch on. Back in the day, I might have put out a cheese board, which is loaded with saturated fat (the cheese, not the board). Or a bowl of chips, which were probably deep-fried in trans fats or saturated fats. No more, though. I have found that the primal urge for salty crunchiness can be handled with more healthful ingredients that are crisped up in just a little oil—all of it of the healthy kind. I've also thrown in my favorite nut butter—made with cashews—and as you'll see, the addition of Parmesan cheese turns it into a delicious savory spread. Yucca, parsnips, and carrots treated like the crispy chips in this chapter are some other vegetables that can make for healthy Happy Hour snacks.

Guacamole with Fresh Corn Chips and Sea Salt | 165

Kale Chips | 166

Beet Chips | 169

Sweet and Spiced Nuts | 170

Roasted Sugar Snaps | 172

Garlic Cashew Butter | 173

Guacamole with Fresh Corn Chips and Sea Salt

We live in an age when everything that can be done to make guacamole different has been tried—from bacon bits, to hard-cooked eggs, to radishes, and even tequila—but as I found when I worked in the Armadillo Café, a small Tex-Mex café in Bay Ridge, Brooklyn, simpler is often better.

For the guacamole, I break up the avocados just enough to make a chunky paste, then hit them immediately with a healthy squeeze of lime juice to keep them nice and green. If you have the time, try charring the jalapeño, which will lend some smokiness to its spicy kick. As for the tortilla chips, I grill them in a little canola oil. The result is more crunch. I think you will also find that more of the flavor of the corn comes through by toasting this way rather than frying.

serves 4

3 avocados, ripe and ready to eat, diced

Juice of 2 limes

2 tablespoons extra virgin olive oil

1 jalapeño chile pepper, seeded and finely chopped (wear plastic gloves when handling)

1 plum tomato, seeded, peeled, and finely chopped

1 teaspoon minced garlic

1½ tablespoons chopped cilantro

Sea salt and fresh ground black pepper to taste

for the chips:

1 package (10-count) fresh corn tortillas

2 tablespoons canola oil

Salt to taste

In a bowl, combine the avocados, lime juice, olive oil, jalapeño pepper, tomato, garlic, cilantro, and sea salt and black pepper. Mash together, leaving some of the avocados in chunks. Set aside.

to make the chips:

Prepare a charcoal grill. Toss the corn tortillas in the oil and grill until blistered on each side. Season with salt. Cut into triangles and serve with the guacamole.

Kale Chips

I don't have many rules in my cooking, but I do believe that if you can make something crisp, people are going to give it a try and probably like it. To my way of thinking, Crispy = Fun. If you told me 10 years ago that people would eat kale for fun, I would have said, "On what planet?" But kale has become a bit of a phenomenon. I love kale chopped up and cooked down with onions and crispy bacon, but for sheer simplicity, it is hard to beat this easy-to-make and easy-to-eat recipe—as irresistible as potato chips but with way less oil.

serves 4

2 pounds kale, thick ribs removed

1 tablespoon olive oil or canola oil

1 teaspoon sea salt

Preheat the oven to 250°F. In a large bowl, toss the kale with the oil to coat the leaves. Season with the sea salt and lay the kale on 2 baking sheets in a single layer. Bake until crisp, about 25 minutes, turning the leaves halfway through.

Beet Chips

Beet chips have a lot more natural sugar than potato chips, but far fewer carbs. The food industry has made a pile by satisfying our lust for potato-chip crispness with "healthier" vegetables instead of potatoes. But there's no need to shell out the big bucks for a few ounces of beet chips when you can make your own so easily and economically. Like the old commercial said, "Bet you can't eat just one!"

serves 4

1½ pounds sugar beets, peeled and thinly sliced on a mandoline

¼ cup canola oil

Salt and fresh ground black pepper to taste

Preheat the oven to 350°F. In a large bowl, toss the beets with the canola oil. Season with the salt and pepper and transfer to 2 baking sheets. Arrange in a single layer. Bake until the beets are wilted, about 20 minutes. Rotate the sheets and bake for 15 minutes. Remove the beets from the baking sheets and place on a cooling rack.

Sweet and Spiced Nuts

I'll admit it. Restaurant owners like to put little nibbles on the bar to stimulate thirst. That's how I started serving these nuts. The inspiration is a mixture of Indian spices, but you could easily go southwestern and use dried chiles and cinnamon. For a Southeast Asian accent, use wasabi paste, sesame seeds, and oil instead of butter. Nuts are so full of flavor and texture that they can accept endless combinations of spices and herbs. This recipe is for 4. It doesn't take a whole lot more time to make a double or triple batch so that you can have this on hand for guests when you feel like having a spontaneous cocktail party. The nuts will keep, tightly covered, in a cool, dry place for up to 2 weeks.

serves 4

---

1 pound walnuts, pecans, or cashews

1 teaspoon kosher salt

½ teaspoon cayenne pepper

½ teaspoon ground cardamom

½ teaspoon ground cinnamon

½ teaspoon ground turmeric

½ teaspoon ground fenugreek

¼ cup unsalted butter, melted

4 tablespoons dark brown sugar

2 tablespoons Sugar in the Raw

2 tablespoons water

Preheat the oven to 350°F. Line a baking sheet with parchment paper. Spread the nuts in a single layer on the baking sheet and toast for 5 minutes. Transfer to a medium bowl. Add the salt, cayenne pepper, cardamom, cinnamon, turmeric, and fenugreek and toss until incorporated. Add the butter, brown sugar, Sugar in the Raw, and water and stir until the nuts are evenly coated. Spread the nuts on the baking sheet and roast until golden brown, stirring twice, about 10 minutes. Separate the nuts with a spatula, taking care not to burn yourself. Transfer to a bowl and serve.

Roasted Sugar Snaps

For kids who say they don't like vegetables, sugar snaps are a foolproof food to make them see the error of their ways. No question they look like a vegetable, but they are as sweet as any fruit and as crunchy as a perfect apple. Roasting concentrates their flavor and brings out their savory side as well. Serve them as a side or as finger food for a little something healthier than a bowl of potato chips.

serves 4

---

1 pound sugar snap peas, strings removed

1 tablespoon extra virgin olive oil

2 sprigs thyme

1 tablespoon sea salt

Fresh ground black pepper to taste

2 tablespoons mint leaves, cut into thin ribbons

Preheat the oven to 450°F. In a bowl, toss the peas with the oil, thyme, and sea salt. Transfer to a baking sheet and arrange in a single layer. Roast until bright green and lightly charred in some areas, about 5 minutes. Remove and discard the thyme. Sprinkle with the pepper, garnish with the mint, and serve.

Garlic Cashew Butter

Nut butters are often quite sweet, but this combination is much more savory. It spreads as easily as butter. You can use it as an hors d'oeuvres, spread on a baguette or pitas. Add Parmesan cheese, which is very high in umami, to pump up the savory taste even more.

serves 4

3 cloves garlic

½ pound roasted unsalted cashews

¼ cup hemp seed oil

1 tablespoon kosher salt

¼ teaspoon cayenne pepper

Preheat the oven to 350°F. Wrap the garlic cloves in foil and roast for 30 minutes. In a blender, combine the cashews, hemp seed oil, garlic, kosher salt, and cayenne pepper. Blend until smooth. The butter will keep, tightly covered, in the refrigerator for up to 2 weeks.

Common Measurements and Equivalents

CONVERSION CHART

These equivalents have been slightly rounded to make measuring easier.

VOLUME MEASUREMENTS			WEIGHT MEASUREMENTS		LENGTH MEASUREMENTS	
U.S.	IMPERIAL	METRIC	U.S.	METRIC	U.S.	METRIC
¼ tsp	–	1 ml	1 oz	30 g	¼"	0.6 cm
½ tsp	–	2 ml	2 oz	60 g	½"	1.25 cm
1 tsp	–	5 ml	4 oz (¼ lb)	115 g	1"	2.5 cm
1 Tbsp	–	15 ml	5 oz (⅓ lb)	145 g	2"	5 cm
2 Tbsp (1 oz)	1 fl oz	30 ml	6 oz	170 g	4"	11 cm
¼ cup (2 oz)	2 fl oz	60 ml	7 oz	200 g	6"	15 cm
⅓ cup (3 oz)	3 fl oz	80 ml	8 oz (½ lb)	230 g	8"	20 cm
½ cup (4 oz)	4 fl oz	120 ml	10 oz	285 g	10"	25 cm
⅔ cup (5 oz)	5 fl oz	160 ml	12 oz (¾ lb)	340 g	12" (1')	30 cm
¾ cup (6 oz)	6 fl oz	180 ml	14 oz	400 g		
1 cup (8 oz)	8 fl oz	240 ml	16 oz (1 lb)	455 g		
			2.2 lb	1 kg		

PAN SIZES		TEMPERATURES		
U.S.	**METRIC**	**FAHRENHEIT**	**CENTIGRADE**	**GAS**
8″ cake pan	20 × 4 cm sandwich or cake tin	140°	60°	–
9″ cake pan	23 × 3.5 cm sandwich or cake tin	160°	70°	–
		180°	80°	–
11″ × 7″ baking pan	28 × 18 cm baking tin	225°	105°	$\frac{1}{4}$
13″ × 9″ baking pan	32.5 × 23 cm baking tin	250°	120°	$\frac{1}{2}$
15″ × 10″ baking pan	38 × 25.5 cm baking tin (Swiss roll tin)	275°	135°	1
		300°	150°	2
1 $\frac{1}{2}$-qt baking dish	1.5-liter baking dish	325°	160°	3
2-qt baking dish	2-liter baking dish	350°	180°	4
2-qt rectangular baking dish	30 × 19 cm baking dish	375°	190°	5
		400°	200°	6
9″ pie plate	22 × 4 or 23 × 4 cm pie plate	425°	220°	7
7″ or 8″ springform pan	18- or 20-cm springform or loose-bottom cake tin	450°	230°	8
		475°	245°	9
9″ × 5″ loaf pan	23 × 13 cm or 2-lb narrow loaf tin or pâté tin	500°	260°	–

Acknowledgments

I would like to thank all those who have helped me with this book:

Rodale Inc. and Editor-at-Large Elissa Altman—for making this book come to life.

Carol Mann—a great book agent and friend for many years. Thank you.

Peter Kaminsky—I couldn't think of a better person to align myself with. You captured me and put my thoughts to paper. You were fun to work with, and I consider you a good friend. Thank you.

Mark Jordan—Quite possibly the best photographer and sous chef I've ever worked with. Mark and I first met in 1999, when he was my sous chef at a restaurant in the city. Mark was an amazing sous chef and worker. He had such dedication. Several years later, Mark reinvented himself as a photographer, photographing, among other things, his true love, food. Mark is able to capture images of the table like no one else. He brings my food to life, and I thank him for that. Mark has been a good friend all these years. It is sincerely my pleasure to have worked with him on this book.

Jonathan Waxman—Thank you so much for your heartfelt Foreword. You are an amazing chef and in so many ways my inspirational force. Your style of cooking is my style of cooking. I think that is why we get along. Your passion is contagious, infectious, and downright beautiful. Thanks, JW!

Lisa Hayim—for assisting Peter and me with nutritional info and more.

Kathleen Hackett—for cleaning up my recipes and making them accessible to the home cook.

Joe Buonnadonna from Samuels & Son Seafood—for the beautiful fish.

Pat La Frieda & Mark Pastore—for the amazing meat.

Cindy, my best friend and partner—Thank you for giving me the strength I needed.

Scott Feldman, the best manager in the business—Thank you for everything you do for me.

To my business partners, John Rigos & Andy Stern, and the entire Aurify Team—Thank you for always being in my corner.

To the Little Beet Team, especially Andrew Duddleston, my partner; Derek Anasiewicz, our GM; and Michael Landas, my longtime sous chef—Thank you for working as hard as you do every day to make the Little Beet what it is, the best healthy fast casual restaurant around.

Mike, Tomas, Neyreda, and Nabor—Without you, I don't think we would get it done as easily. You are the best kitchen team ever assembled.

Charlie, Jesse, Kate, and JJ (Team DOOR)—for being the best PR team and helping direct my career.

Index

Underscored page references indicate sidebars. **Boldface** references indicate photographs.

A

Acids, for enhancing flavor, xxx
Acorn squash
    Acorn Squash, Hazelnuts, Parmesan, and Acacia Honey, 146, **147**
    Acorn Squash Soup with Pistachios, Black Bread, and Apples, 28, **29**
Agrumato
    Mackerel, Oranges, Mint, Chiles, and Lemon Agrumato, **84**, 85
Almonds
    Almond-Dusted Chicken Breasts, 105
    Banana and Almond Freeze, 157
    Cauliflower-Leek Soup with Madras Curry and Almonds, 27
    food combinations with, xxxii
    Toasted Almond Quinoa Pilaf, 41
Apples
    Acorn Squash Soup with Pistachios, Black Bread, and Apples, 28, **29**
    Baked Apples with Walnuts and Raisins, 156
    Baked Sweet Potatoes, Granny Smith Apples, Chives, and Walnuts, 140
    Curried Beets, Apple, Fried Shallots, and Walnuts, 121
    Radish, Apple, Hazelnut, and Arugula Salad, 21
Arteries, effect of fat on, xvi
Arugula
    Grilled Portobello Mushroom Sandwiches with Arugula and Date-Walnut Pesto, 134
    Quinoa, Beet, and Arugula Salad, 37
    Radish, Apple, Hazelnut, and Arugula Salad, 21
    Salmon, Grapefruit, Olive Oil, and Arugula, 76
Asian-style dishes
    Pan-Roasted Brussels Sprouts with Southeast Asian Flavors, 128, **129**
    Tokyo/Vietnam Tuna Wrap, 80
Autism, food sensitivities with, xix, xxii
Avocados
    attributes of, xx, xxii
    Avocado Ice Cream with Lime and Coconut, **160**, 161
    Beets with Avocado and Kefir, 6
    Ceviche of Snapper with Avocado and Cilantro, **56**, 57
    Five Fat Challenge: Salmon Avocado Caponata with Pistachios and Black Olive Oil, **78**, 79
    Grilled Salmon, Lentils, Avocado, and Pecans, with Sherry Vinaigrette, 77
    Grilled Shrimp with Black Quinoa, Avocado, and Oranges, 60, **61**
    Grilled Turkey, Avocado, and Tomato on Seven Grain, 106
    Guacamole with Fresh Corn Chips and Sea Salt, 165
    healthy fat in, xvii, xix, xx
    Heirloom Tomatoes, Avocado, Mango, and Cucumber, 8, **9**
    Lentils, Avocado, Oranges, Pecans, and Kale with Ginger Dressing, 16, **17**
    Puffed Millet, Tomatoes, Jalapeño, and Avocado, **46**, 47
    Roasted Carrots with Cumin and Avocado, 150
    uses for, xx

B

Bananas
    Banana and Almond Freeze, 157
Barbecue sauce
    Barbecue Chicken Wraps with Celery and Bean Sprouts, 104
Barley
    Barley with Onions and Pine Nuts, 44
Barley noodles
    Barley Noodles in Mushroom and Onion Broth, 45
Beans, xxxiii
    Chorizo and Chickpeas with Charred Onions, Black Olives, and Herbs, **114**, 115
    Grilled Shrimp Arrabbiata with Chickpeas and Broccoli, 59
    Squid Confit with White Bean Stifado, 69
    Tons of Crunch Summer Bean Salad, 7
Bean sprouts
    Barbecue Chicken Wraps with Celery and Bean Sprouts, 104
Becker, Franklin
    cooking style of, ix–xii
    on creating healthy flavors, xxiii–xxiv
    culinary journey of, xvii–xx
    diabetes cookbooks of, xviii, xxii
    favorite go-to ingredients of, xxvii–xxviii, xxx–xxxiii
    favorite healthy fats of, xx, xxii
    on portion sizes, xxiv–xxv
Beef
    Beef Tartare with Capers, Pistachio Pesto, and Watermelon-Tomato Salad, 107–8, **109**
    Grilled Skirt Steak with Warm Potato Salad and Chimichurri, 110
Beets
    Baby Beets with Goat Cheese and Fennel, **4**, 5
    Beet Chips, **168**, 169
    Beets, Goat Cheese, and Crunchy Herb Salad, 3
    Beets with Avocado and Kefir, 6
    Curried Beets, Apple, Fried Shallots, and Walnuts, 121
    Quinoa, Beet, and Arugula Salad, 37

Black quinoa, x
    Black Quinoa with Pine Nuts,
        Scallions, and Oranges, with
        Ginger Dressing, 40
    Grilled Shrimp with Black Quinoa,
        Avocado, and Oranges, 60, **61**
Boudin
    Seafood Boudin, 70–71
Bread
    Acorn Squash Soup with Pistachios,
        Black Bread, and Apples, 28, **29**
    Grilled Turkey, Avocado, and
        Tomato on Seven Grain, 106
Broccoli
    Blistered Broccoli with Garlic and
        Chiles, 131, **132–33**
    Broiled Local Flounder Oreganata
        with Charred Broccoli, 94
    Grilled Shrimp Arrabbiata with
        Chickpeas and Broccoli, 59
    Sautéed Broccoli with Garlic and
        Chiles, 130
Brussels sprouts
    Autumn on a Plate, 12, **13**
    Pan-Roasted Brussels Sprouts
        with Southeast Asian Flavors,
        128, **129**
Buckwheat, as gluten-free food, xix
Butter
    occasional eating of, xviii
    saturated fat in, xvi
Butternut squash
    Butternut Squash Soup with Walnut
        Pesto, 30, 31

C

Cake
    Maria's Ravani, 159
Calories
    excess, obesity from, xv–xvi
    in nuts, xxii
Capers
    Beef Tartare with Capers, Pistachio
        Pesto, and Watermelon-
        Tomato Salad, 107–8, **109**
Caponata
    Five Fat Challenge: Salmon Avocado
        Caponata with Pistachios and
        Black Olive Oil, 78, **79**
Cara Cara oranges
    Grilled Shrimp with Black Quinoa,
        Avocado, and Oranges, 60, **61**
    Mackerel, Oranges, Mint, Chiles, and
        Lemon Agrumato, **84**, 85
    Shrimp Semi-Ceviche Cara Cara, 65

Carbohydrates, function of, xv
Carrots
    Carrot and Ginger Soup, 32
    Roasted Carrots with Cumin and
        Avocado, 150
    Roasted Carrots with Sumac,
        Lemon, and Honey,
        148, 149
Cashews
    Cashew Panna Cotta with Tropical
        Fruit, 154, **155**
    food combinations with, xxxii
    Garlic Cashew Butter, 173
    Sweet and Spiced Nuts, 170, **171**
Cauliflower
    Cauliflower Couscous with Fresh
        Herbs, Currants, and Coconut,
        120
    Cauliflower-Leek Soup with Madras
        Curry and Almonds, 27
Celery
    Barbecue Chicken Wraps with
        Celery and Bean Sprouts, 104
Ceviche
    Ceviche of Snapper with Avocado
        and Cilantro, 56, 57
    Shrimp Semi-Ceviche Cara Cara, 65
Cheeses
    Acorn Squash, Hazelnuts, Parmesan,
        and Acacia Honey, 146, **147**
    Baby Beets with Goat Cheese and
        Fennel, 4, 5
    Beets, Goat Cheese, and Crunchy
        Herb Salad, 3
    Caramelized Sweet Potatoes with
        Smoked Sea Salt and
        Pecorino, 138, **139**
    Fresh Ricotta with Figs, Olive Oil,
        and Chili Flakes, **18–19**, 20
    Kale Salad with Pecorino Cheese,
        Pumpkin Seeds, and Grapes,
        14, 15
    occasional eating of, xviii
    Quinoa, Feta Cheese, Raisins, and
        Pistachios, 42, **43**
    Quinoa Tabbouleh with Feta Cheese
        and Cucumber, **38**, 39
Chicken
    Almond-Dusted Chicken Breasts,
        105
    Barbecue Chicken Wraps with
        Celery and Bean Sprouts, 104
    Grilled Chicken with Ramp Pesto,
        101, **102–3**

Grilled Chicken with Tomato Jam,
        100
    Slow-Roasted Organic Chicken with
        Parsley, Sage, Rosemary, and
        Thyme, 98, **99**
Chickpeas
    Chorizo and Chickpeas with Charred
        Onions, Black Olives, and
        Herbs, **114**, 115
    Grilled Shrimp Arrabbiata with
        Chickpeas and Broccoli, 59
Chile peppers
    Baby Lamb Chops with Chili,
        Mint, and Provençal
        Marinade, 111
    Blistered Broccoli with Garlic and
        Chiles, 131, **132–33**
    Fresh Ricotta with Figs,
        Olive Oil, and Chili Flakes,
        18–19, 20
    Grilled Sea Bass with Spigarello,
        Chiles, and Garlic, 89
    Mackerel, Oranges, Mint, Chiles, and
        Lemon Agrumato, **84**, 85
    Puffed Millet, Tomatoes, Jalapeño,
        and Avocado, **46**, 47
    Sautéed Broccoli with Garlic and
        Chiles, 130
Chimichurri
    Grilled Skirt Steak with Warm Potato
        Salad and Chimichurri, 110
Chips
    Beet Chips, **168**, 169
    Guacamole with Fresh Corn Chips
        and Sea Salt, 165
    Kale Chips, 166, **167**
Chives
    Baked Sweet Potatoes, Granny
        Smith Apples, Chives, and
        Walnuts, 140
    Tuna Cubes with Citrus Soy, Chives,
        and Cucumber, 82, **83**
Cholesterol, LDL, nuts lowering, xxii
Chorizo
    Chorizo and Chickpeas with Charred
        Onions, Black Olives, and
        Herbs, **114**, 115
Cilantro
    Ceviche of Snapper with Avocado
        and Cilantro, 56, 57
Clams
    Clams Steamed in Sake with Soy
        and Pine Nuts, 66, **67**
    Stewed Clams and Mussels with
        Garlic and Vinho Verde, 68

Coconut
    Avocado Ice Cream with Lime and
        Coconut, **160**, 161
    Cauliflower Couscous with Fresh
        Herbs, Currants, and Coconut,
        120
    Coconut- and Macadamia-Dusted
        Shrimp with Tropical Fruit
        Salad, **62**, 63–64
Cod
    Olive Oil–Poached Cod with
        Roasted Tomato and Peppers,
        86, **87**, 88
Cookies
    Date and Walnut Cookies, 158
Corn chips
    Guacamole with Fresh Corn Chips
        and Sea Salt, 165
Crab
    Seafood Boudin, 70–71
Cucumbers
    Heirloom Tomatoes, Avocado,
        Mango, and Cucumber, 8, **9**
    Quinoa Tabbouleh with Feta Cheese
        and Cucumber, **38**, 39
    Strawberries, Fennel, and Cucumber
        Salad, **10**, 11
    Tuna Cubes with Citrus Soy, Chives,
        and Cucumber, 82, **83**
Cumin
    Roasted Carrots with Cumin and
        Avocado, 150
Currants
    Cauliflower Couscous with Fresh
        Herbs, Currants, and Coconut,
        120
Curry powder. *See* Madras curry

D

Dates
    Date and Walnut Cookies, 158
    Grilled Portobello Mushroom
        Sandwiches with Arugula and
        Date-Walnut Pesto, 134
Desserts, 151, 153
    Avocado Ice Cream with Lime and
        Coconut, **160**, 161
    Baked Apples with Walnuts and
        Raisins, 156
    Banana and Almond Freeze, 157
    Cashew Panna Cotta with Tropical
        Fruit, 154, **155**

Date and Walnut Cookies, 158
Maria's Ravani, 159
Diabetes, xvii–xviii
Diabetes cookbooks, xviii, xxii

E

Eggplant
    Blistered Fairytale Eggplant Stewed
        in Olive Oil, Cherry Tomatoes,
        and Herbs, 123
    Charred Eggplant, Grilled Onions,
        Pickled Raisins, and Pine
        Nuts, 122
    Five Fat Challenge: Salmon Avocado
        Caponata with Pistachios and
        Black Olive Oil, **78**, 79

F

Farro
    Farro Salad with Pickled
        Mushrooms, Golden Raisins,
        and Tender Greens, 48, **49**
Fats, dietary
    from free-ranging, grass-fed
        animals, <u>xviii</u>
    functions of, xv, xvi–xvii, 1
    healthy
        author's discovery of, xix–xx
        author's favorite, xx, xxii
        misunderstanding of, xv
        in nuts, xvi, xix, xxii
        in oils, xxxii
        in salads, 1
        in seafood, xxii, xxiii, 51
        in soups, 23
    monounsaturated, <u>xviii</u>, xix, xx, 95
    saturated, xvi, 95
    trans fat, xvi
    types used in recipes, xvi
    unsaturated, xvi, xix
Fennel
    Baby Beets with Goat Cheese and
        Fennel, **4**, 5
    Slow-Cooked Fennel in Olive Oil,
        125, **126–27**
    Strawberries, Fennel, and Cucumber
        Salad, **10**, 11
Feta cheese
    Quinoa, Feta Cheese, Raisins, and
        Pistachios, 42, **43**
    Quinoa Tabbouleh with Feta Cheese
        and Cucumber, **38**, 39

Figs
    Fresh Ricotta with Figs, Olive Oil,
        and Chili Flakes, **18–19**, 20
Fish. *See* Seafood, fish
Flavoring blends, author's favorite, xxxi
Flavor(s)
    choosing ingredients for,
        xxiii–xxiv
    fat enhancing, xvi–xvii
    ingredients enhancing,
        xxvii–xxviii, xxx–xxxiii
    regional influences on, xvii, xix
Flay, Bobby, ix, xvii
Flounder
    Broiled Local Flounder Oreganata
        with Charred Broccoli, 94
Flours, nut-based, xix
Fries
    Pumpkin Fries, 145
Fruits. *See also specific fruits*
    Cashew Panna Cotta with Tropical
        Fruit, 154, **155**
    Coconut- and Macadamia-Dusted
        Shrimp with Tropical Fruit
        Salad, **62**, 63–64

G

Garam masala, xxx
Garlic
    Gambas al Ajillo (Shrimp with Garlic
        and Oil), 58
    Garlic Cashew Butter, 173
    Grilled Sea Bass with Spigarello,
        Chiles, and Garlic, 89
    Peppers Stewed in Olive Oil, Herbs,
        and Garlic, 124
    Rock Lobster Tails with Garlic and
        Oil, **72**, 73
    Sautéed Broccoli with Garlic and
        Chiles, 130
    Stewed Clams and Mussels with
        Garlic and Vinho Verde, 68
Ginger
    Black Quinoa with Pine Nuts,
        Scallions, and Oranges, with
        Ginger Dressing, 40
    Carrot and Ginger Soup, 32
    Lentils, Avocado, Oranges, Pecans,
        and Kale with Ginger Dressing,
        16, **17**
Ginger juice, how to make, 16
Gluten-free grains or grain substitutes,
    xix, 33
Gluten sensitivity, with autism, xix

Goat cheese
    Baby Beets with Goat Cheese and
        Fennel, **4**, 5
    Beets, Goat Cheese, and Crunchy
        Herb Salad, 3
Gottschall, Elaine, xxii
Grains, x, xxxiii, 33, **34**, 35
    Barley Noodles in Mushroom and
        Onion Broth, 45
    Barley with Onions and Pine Nuts,
        44
    Black Quinoa with Pine Nuts,
        Scallions, and Oranges, with
        Ginger Dressing, 40
    Farro Salad with Pickled
        Mushrooms, Golden Raisins,
        and Tender Greens, 48, **49**
    gluten-free, xix, 33
    Puffed Millet, Tomatoes, Jalapeño,
        and Avocado, **46**, 47
    Quinoa, Beet, and Arugula Salad, 37
    Quinoa, Feta Cheese, Raisins, and
        Pistachios, 42, **43**
    Quinoa Tabbouleh with Feta Cheese
        and Cucumber, **38**, 39
    Toasted Almond Quinoa Pilaf, 41
    Toasted Kasha with Mushrooms and
        Scallions, 36
    Wild Rice Salad with Kale, Pecans,
        and Oranges, 50
Grapefruit
    Salmon, Grapefruit, Olive Oil, and
        Arugula, 76
Grapes
    Kale Salad with Pecorino Cheese,
        Pumpkin Seeds, and Grapes,
        14, 15
Greek-style dishes
    Grilled Octopus Greek Style, 74, **75**
    Quinoa, Feta Cheese, Raisins, and
        Pistachios, 42, **43**
    Squid Confit with White Bean
        Stifado, 69
Greens
    Farro Salad with Pickled
        Mushrooms, Golden Raisins,
        and Tender Greens, 48, **49**
Gremolata
    Grilled Sea Bream with Lemon
        Gremolata and Spinach, 90, **91**
Grimes, Bill, xxiii–xxiv
Guacamole
    Guacamole with Fresh Corn Chips
        and Sea Salt, 165

H

Hazelnuts
    Acorn Squash, Hazelnuts, Parmesan,
        and Acacia Honey, 146, **147**
    food combinations with, xxxii
    Radish, Apple, Hazelnut, and
        Arugula Salad, 21
Heart disease, fats linked to, xvi
Herbs. *See also specific herbs*
    Beets, Goat Cheese, and Crunchy
        Herb Salad, 3
    Blistered Fairytale Eggplant Stewed
        in Olive Oil, Cherry Tomatoes,
        and Herbs, 123
    Cauliflower Couscous with Fresh
        Herbs, Currants, and Coconut,
        120
    Chorizo and Chickpeas with Charred
        Onions, Black Olives, and
        Herbs, **114**, 115
    Pan-Roasted Mushrooms, Herbs,
        and Spices, 135
    Peppers Stewed in Olive Oil, Herbs,
        and Garlic, 124
    for savoriness, xxviii
Honey
    Acorn Squash, Hazelnuts, Parmesan,
        and Acacia Honey, 146, **147**
    Roasted Carrots with Sumac,
        Lemon, and Honey, **148**, 149

I

Ice cream
    Avocado Ice Cream with Lime and
        Coconut, **160**, 161
Ingredients
    best, finding, xi, xxiii–xxiv
    for best flavor, xix, xxiv
    for enhancing flavor,
        xxvii–xxviii, xxx–xxxiii
    swapping, xi
    tasting, in dishes, xii, xxiii

J

Jalapeño chile pepper
    Puffed Millet, Tomatoes, Jalapeño,
        and Avocado, **46**, 47
Jam
    Grilled Chicken with Tomato Jam,
        100

K

Kabocha squash
    Autumn on a Plate, 12, **13**
Kale
    Kale Chips, 166, **167**
    Kale Salad with Pecorino Cheese,
        Pumpkin Seeds, and Grapes,
        14, 15
    Lentils, Avocado, Oranges, Pecans,
        and Kale with Ginger Dressing,
        16, **17**
    Wild Rice Salad with Kale, Pecans,
        and Oranges, 50
Kasha
    Toasted Kasha with Mushrooms and
        Scallions, 36
Kefir
    Beets with Avocado and Kefir, 6
Kosher salt, xxxii

L

Lamb
    Baby Lamb Chops with Chili, Mint,
        and Provençal Marinade, 111
    Oven-Roasted Lamb Shoulder, 112,
        113
LDL cholesterol, nuts lowering, xxii
Leeks
    Cauliflower-Leek Soup with Madras
        Curry and Almonds, 27
Leftovers, xxv
Lemons
    for enhancing flavor, xxx
    Grilled Sea Bream with Lemon
        Gremolata and Spinach, 90, **91**
    Mackerel, Oranges, Mint, Chiles, and
        Lemon Agrumato, **84**, 85
    Roasted Carrots with Sumac,
        Lemon, and Honey, **148**, 149
Lentils
    Grilled Salmon, Lentils, Avocado,
        and Pecans, with Sherry
        Vinaigrette, 77
    Lentils, Avocado, Oranges, Pecans,
        and Kale with Ginger Dressing,
        16, **17**
Le Sirenuse restaurant, x, xviii–xix
Limes
    Avocado Ice Cream with Lime and
        Coconut, **160**, 161
    for enhancing flavor, xxx

Lobster
    Rock Lobster Tails with Garlic and
        Oil, **72**, 73

M

Macadamia nuts
    Coconut- and Macadamia-Dusted
        Shrimp with Tropical Fruit
        Salad, **62**, 63–64
Mackerel. *See* Spanish mackerel
Madras curry, xxx
    Cauliflower-Leek Soup with Madras
        Curry and Almonds, 27
    Curried Beets, Apple, Fried Shallots,
        and Walnuts, 121
Mangoes
    Cashew Panna Cotta with Tropical
        Fruit, 154, **155**
    Heirloom Tomatoes, Avocado,
        Mango, and Cucumber, 8, **9**
Marinade
    Baby Lamb Chops with Chili, Mint,
        and Provençal Marinade, 111
Mayonnaise
    Spicy Eggless Mayo, 71
Meats, 97. *See also* Beef; Lamb;
        Sausage
    fat in, 95
    from free-ranging, grass-fed
        animals, <u>xviii</u>, 95
    serving size of, 95
Mediterranean diet, x–xi, xix
Millet
    Puffed Millet, Tomatoes, Jalapeño,
        and Avocado, **46**, 47
Mint
    Baby Lamb Chops with Chili, Mint,
        and Provençal Marinade, 111
    Mackerel, Oranges, Mint, Chiles, and
        Lemon Agrumato, **84**, 85
Miso
    Charred String Beans with Tofu-
        Miso Dressing, **136**, 137
Monounsaturated fats, sources of, <u>xviii</u>,
        xix, xx, 95
Mouth feel, xvi, xx, xxxii, 23
Mushrooms
    Barley Noodles in Mushroom and
        Onion Broth, 45
    Farro Salad with Pickled
        Mushrooms, Golden Raisins,
        and Tender Greens, 48, **49**

Grilled Portobello Mushroom
        Sandwiches with Arugula and
        Date-Walnut Pesto, 134
    Pan-Roasted Mushrooms, Herbs,
        and Spices, 135
    Toasted Kasha with Mushrooms and
        Scallions, 36
Mussels
    Stewed Clams and Mussels with
        Garlic and Vinho Verde, 68
Mustard greens
    Autumn on a Plate, 12, **13**

N

Nestle, Marion, xv
Nut butter
    Garlic Cashew Butter, 173
Nutrition transition, 95
Nuts. *See also* Almonds; Cashews;
        Hazelnuts; Macadamia nuts;
        Pecans; Pine nuts; Pistachios;
        Walnuts
    attributes of, xix, xx, xxii, xxxii
    food combinations with, xxxii
    Sweet and Spiced Nuts, 170, **171**
    unsaturated fat in, xvi, xix, xxii

O

Obesity
    contributors to, xv–xvi, xxiv, 95
    diabetes from, xvii
Octopus
    Grilled Octopus Greek Style, 74, **75**
Oils, with healthy fat, xxxii
Olive oil
    attributes of, x, xix, xx
    Blistered Fairytale Eggplant Stewed
        in Olive Oil, Cherry Tomatoes,
        and Herbs, 123
    Five Fat Challenge: Salmon Avocado
        Caponata with Pistachios and
        Black Olive Oil, **78**, 79
    Fresh Ricotta with Figs, Olive Oil,
        and Chili Flakes, **18–19**, 20
    Gambas al Ajillo (Shrimp with Garlic
        and Oil), 58
    Mackerel, Oranges, Mint, Chiles, and
        Lemon Agrumato, **84**, 85

Olive Oil–Poached Cod with
        Roasted Tomato and Peppers,
        86, **87**, 88
    Peppers Stewed in Olive Oil, Herbs,
        and Garlic, 124
    Rock Lobster Tails with Garlic and
        Oil, **72**, 73
    Salmon, Grapefruit, Olive Oil, and
        Arugula, 76
    Slow-Cooked Fennel in Olive Oil,
        125, **126–27**
    unsaturated fat in, xvi
Olives
    Chorizo and Chickpeas with Charred
        Onions, Black Olives, and
        Herbs, **114**, 115
    Grilled Spanish Mackerel with Black
        Olives, Tomatoes, and Pistou,
        81
Omega-3 fatty acids, xvi
    in fish, xxii, 51
Omega-6 fatty acids, xvi
Onions
    Barley Noodles in Mushroom and
        Onion Broth, 45
    Barley with Onions and Pine Nuts,
        44
    Charred Eggplant, Grilled Onions,
        Pickled Raisins, and Pine Nuts,
        122
    Chorizo and Chickpeas with Charred
        Onions, Black Olives, and
        Herbs, **114**, 115
Oranges
    Black Quinoa with Pine Nuts,
        Scallions, and Oranges, with
        Ginger Dressing, 40
    for enhancing flavor, xxx
    Grilled Shrimp with Black Quinoa,
        Avocado, and Oranges, 60, **61**
    Lentils, Avocado, Oranges, Pecans,
        and Kale with Ginger Dressing,
        16, **17**
    Mackerel, Oranges, Mint, Chiles, and
        Lemon Agrumato, **84**, 85
    Shrimp Semi-Ceviche Cara Cara, 65
    Wild Rice Salad with Kale, Pecans,
        and Oranges, 50
Oregano
    Broiled Local Flounder Oreganata
        with Charred Broccoli, 94
Overweight
    causes of, xv–xvi
    health problems from, xv

P

Panna cotta
 Cashew Panna Cotta with Tropical
  Fruit, 154, **155**
Papaya
 Cashew Panna Cotta with Tropical
  Fruit, 154, **155**
Parmesan cheese
 Acorn Squash, Hazelnuts, Parmesan,
  and Acacia Honey, 146, **147**
Parsley
 Grilled Skirt Steak with Warm Potato
  Salad and Chimichurri, 110
 Slow-Roasted Organic Chicken with
  Parsley, Sage, Rosemary, and
  Thyme, 98, **99**
Peanuts, food combinations with, xxxii
Pecans
 food combinations with, xxxii
 Grilled Salmon, Lentils, Avocado,
  and Pecans, with Sherry
  Vinaigrette, 77
 Lentils, Avocado, Oranges, Pecans,
  and Kale with Ginger Dressing,
  16, **17**
 Sweet and Spiced Nuts, 170, **171**
 Wild Rice Salad with Kale, Pecans,
  and Oranges, 50
Pecorino cheese
 Caramelized Sweet Potatoes with
  Smoked Sea Salt and
  Pecorino, 138, **139**
 Kale Salad with Pecorino Cheese,
  Pumpkin Seeds, and Grapes,
  14, 15
Peppers, bell
 Grilled Striped Bass with Sweet
  Peppers, New Potatoes, and
  Pesto, **92**, 93
 Olive Oil–Poached Cod with
  Roasted Tomato and Peppers,
  86, **87**, 88
 Peppers Stewed in Olive Oil, Herbs,
  and Garlic, 124
Peppers, chile. *See* Chile peppers
Pesto
 Beef Tartare with Capers, Pistachio
  Pesto, and Watermelon-
  Tomato Salad, 107–8, **109**
 Butternut Squash Soup with Walnut
  Pesto, 30, **31**
 Grilled Chicken with Ramp Pesto,
  101, **102–3**

Grilled Chicken with Tomato Jam,
 100
Grilled Portobello Mushroom
 Sandwiches with Arugula and
 Date-Walnut Pesto, 134
Grilled Striped Bass with Sweet
 Peppers, New Potatoes, and
 Pesto, **92**, 93
Pickling spice, xxx
Pilaf
 Toasted Almond Quinoa Pilaf, 41
Pineapple
 Cashew Panna Cotta with Tropical
  Fruit, 154, **155**
Pine nuts
 Barley with Onions and Pine Nuts,
  44
 Black Quinoa with Pine Nuts,
  Scallions, and Oranges, with
  Ginger Dressing, 40
 Charred Eggplant, Grilled Onions,
  Pickled Raisins, and Pine
  Nuts, 122
 Clams Steamed in Sake with Soy
  and Pine Nuts, **66**, 67
 food combinations with, xxxii
Pistachios
 Acorn Squash Soup with
  Pistachios, Black Bread, and
  Apples, 28, **29**
 Beef Tartare with Capers, Pistachio
  Pesto, and Watermelon-
  Tomato Salad, 107–8, **109**
 Five Fat Challenge: Salmon Avocado
  Caponata with Pistachios and
  Black Olive Oil, **78**, 79
 food combinations with, xxxii
 Quinoa, Feta Cheese, Raisins, and
  Pistachios, 42, **43**
Pistou
 Grilled Spanish Mackerel with
  Black Olives, Tomatoes, and
  Pistou, 81
Portion sizes, xviii, xix, xxiv–xxv, 95
Portuguese-style dish
 Portuguese Potatoes, **142**, 143
Potatoes
 Grilled Skirt Steak with Warm Potato
  Salad and Chimichurri, 110
 Grilled Striped Bass with Sweet
  Peppers, New Potatoes, and
  Pesto, **92**, 93
 Portuguese Potatoes, **142**, 143
 Spice-Dusted Potatoes, 144

Poultry, 97. *See also* Chicken; Turkey
 saturated fat in, 95
 serving size of, 95
Protein, function of, xv
Pumpkin
 Pumpkin Fries, 145
Pumpkin seeds
 food combinations with, xxxii
 Kale Salad with Pecorino Cheese,
  Pumpkin Seeds, and Grapes,
  14, 15

Q

Quinoa, x, 33
 Black Quinoa with Pine Nuts,
  Scallions, and Oranges, with
  Ginger Dressing, 40
 as gluten-free food, xix
 Grilled Shrimp with Black Quinoa,
  Avocado, and Oranges, 60, **61**
 Quinoa, Beet, and Arugula Salad, 37
 Quinoa, Feta Cheese, Raisins, and
  Pistachios, 42, **43**
 Quinoa Tabbouleh with Feta Cheese
  and Cucumber, **38**, 39
 Toasted Almond Quinoa Pilaf, 41

R

Radishes
 Radish, Apple, Hazelnut, and
  Arugula Salad, 21
Raisins
 Baked Apples with Walnuts and
  Raisins, 156
 Charred Eggplant, Grilled Onions,
  Pickled Raisins, and Pine
  Nuts, 122
 Farro Salad with Pickled
  Mushrooms, Golden Raisins,
  and Tender Greens, 48, **49**
 Quinoa, Feta Cheese, Raisins, and
  Pistachios, 42, **43**
Ramps
 Grilled Chicken with Ramp Pesto,
  101, **102–3**
Ravani
 Maria's Ravani, 159
Recipes
 flavorful ingredients for, xxiii–xxiv
 portion sizes of, xxiv–xxv
 types of fat used in, xvi

Ricotta cheese
    Fresh Ricotta with Figs, Olive Oil,
        and Chili Flakes, **18–19**, 20
Rosemary
    Slow-Roasted Organic Chicken with
        Parsley, Sage, Rosemary, and
        Thyme, 98, **99**

S

Sage
    Slow-Roasted Organic Chicken with
        Parsley, Sage, Rosemary, and
        Thyme, 98, **99**
Sake
    Clams Steamed in Sake with Soy
        and Pine Nuts, **66**, 67
Salads, 2
    Autumn on a Plate, 12, **13**
    Baby Beets with Goat Cheese and
        Fennel, **4**, 5
    Barley with Onions and Pine Nuts,
        44
    Beef Tartare with Capers, Pistachio
        Pesto, and Watermelon-
        Tomato Salad, 107–8, **109**
    Beets, Goat Cheese, and Crunchy
        Herb Salad, 3
    Beets with Avocado and Kefir, 6
    Coconut- and Macadamia-Dusted
        Shrimp with Tropical Fruit
        Salad, 62, **63–64**
    components of, 1
    Farro Salad with Pickled
        Mushrooms, Golden Raisins,
        and Tender Greens, 48, **49**
    Fresh Ricotta with Figs, Olive Oil,
        and Chili Flakes, **18–19**, 20
    Grilled Shrimp with Black Quinoa,
        Avocado, and Oranges, 60, **61**
    Grilled Skirt Steak with Warm Potato
        Salad and Chimichurri, 110
    Heirloom Tomatoes, Avocado,
        Mango, and Cucumber, 8, **9**
    Kale Salad with Pecorino Cheese,
        Pumpkin Seeds, and Grapes,
        14, 15
    Lentils, Avocado, Oranges, Pecans,
        and Kale with Ginger Dressing,
        16, **17**
    nuts in, xix
    oil enhancing, xvi–xvii
    Quinoa, Beet, and Arugula Salad, 37

Quinoa, Feta Cheese, Raisins, and
    Pistachios, 42, **43**
Quinoa Tabbouleh with Feta Cheese
    and Cucumber, **38**, 39
Radish, Apple, Hazelnut, and
    Arugula Salad, 21
Strawberries, Fennel, and Cucumber
    Salad, **10**, 11
Tons of Crunch Summer Bean Salad, 7
Wild Rice Salad with Kale, Pecans,
    and Oranges, 50
Salmon
    Five Fat Challenge: Salmon Avocado
        Caponata with Pistachios and
        Black Olive Oil, **78**, 79
    Grilled Salmon, Lentils, Avocado,
        and Pecans, with Sherry
        Vinaigrette, 77
    Salmon, Grapefruit, Olive Oil, and
        Arugula, 76
Salts, for seasoning, xxxii. *See also* Sea
    salt
Sandwiches. *See also* Wraps
    Grilled Portobello Mushroom
        Sandwiches with Arugula and
        Date-Walnut Pesto, 134
Satiety, from nuts, xxii
Saturated fat
    in butter, xvi
    in meat, 95
Sausage
    Chorizo and Chickpeas with Charred
        Onions, Black Olives, and
        Herbs, **114**, 115
Scallions
    Black Quinoa with Pine Nuts,
        Scallions, and Oranges, with
        Ginger Dressing, 40
    Toasted Kasha with Mushrooms and
        Scallions, 36
Scallops
    Shrimp Semi-Ceviche Cara Cara, 65
Sea bass
    Grilled Sea Bass with Spigarello,
        Chiles, and Garlic, 89
Sea bream
    Grilled Sea Bream with Lemon
        Gremolata and Spinach, 90, **91**
Seafood, 51, **52–53**, 54–55
    fish
        Broiled Local Flounder Oreganata
            with Charred Broccoli, 94
        Ceviche of Snapper with
            Avocado and Cilantro, **56**, 57

Five Fat Challenge: Salmon
    Avocado Caponata with
    Pistachios and Black Olive Oil,
    78, 79
Grilled Salmon, Lentils, Avocado,
    and Pecans, with Sherry
    Vinaigrette, 77
Grilled Sea Bass with Spigarello,
    Chiles, and Garlic, 89
Grilled Sea Bream with Lemon
    Gremolata and Spinach, 90, **91**
Grilled Spanish Mackerel with
    Black Olives, Tomatoes, and
    Pistou, 81
Grilled Striped Bass with Sweet
    Peppers, New Potatoes, and
    Pesto, **92**, 93
healthy fat in, xxii, xxiii
Mackerel, Oranges, Mint,
    Chiles, and Lemon
    Agrumato, **84**, 85
Olive Oil–Poached Cod with
    Roasted Tomato and Peppers,
    86, **87**, 88
protein in, xxii
Salmon, Grapefruit, Olive Oil, and
    Arugula, 76
sustainable varieties of, xxii
Tokyo/Vietnam Tuna Wrap, 80
Tuna Cubes with Citrus Soy,
    Chives, and Cucumber, 82, **83**
shellfish
    Clams Steamed in Sake with Soy
        and Pine Nuts, **66**, 67
    Coconut- and Macadamia-
        Dusted Shrimp with Tropical
        Fruit Salad, 62, **63–64**
    Gambas al Ajillo (Shrimp with
        Garlic and Oil), 58
    Grilled Octopus Greek Style, 74, **75**
    Grilled Shrimp Arrabbiata with
        Chickpeas and Broccoli, 59
    Grilled Shrimp with Black Quinoa,
        Avocado, and Oranges, 60, **61**
    protein in, xxii
    Rock Lobster Tails with Garlic and
        Oil, **72**, 73
    Seafood Boudin, 70–71
    Shrimp Semi-Ceviche Cara Cara,
        65
    Squid Confit with White Bean
        Stifado, 69
    Stewed Clams and Mussels with
        Garlic and Vinho Verde, 68

Sea salt, xxxii
    Caramelized Sweet Potatoes with
        Smoked Sea Salt and
        Pecorino, 138, **139**
    Guacamole with Fresh Corn Chips
        and Sea Salt, 165
Sesame seeds, food combinations
        with, xxxii
Shallots
    Curried Beets, Apple, Fried Shallots,
        and Walnuts, 121
Shellfish. *See* Seafood, shellfish
Shrimp
    Coconut- and Macadamia-Dusted
        Shrimp with Tropical Fruit
        Salad, **62**, 63–64
    Gambas al Ajillo (Shrimp with Garlic
        and Oil), 58
    Grilled Shrimp Arrabbiata with
        Chickpeas and Broccoli, 59
    Grilled Shrimp with Black Quinoa,
        Avocado, and Oranges, 60, **61**
    Seafood Boudin, 70–71
    Shrimp Semi-Ceviche Cara Cara, 65
Simple cooking and food, ix
Snacks, **162**, 163, 164
    Beet Chips, **168**, 169
    Garlic Cashew Butter, 173
    Guacamole with Fresh Corn Chips
        and Sea Salt, 165
    Kale Chips, 166, **167**
    Roasted Sugar Snaps, 172
    Sweet and Spiced Nuts, 170, **171**
Snapper
    Ceviche of Snapper with Avocado
        and Cilantro, **56**, 57
Soups, 23–24
    Acorn Squash Soup with Pistachios,
        Black Bread, and Apples, 28, **29**
    Butternut Squash Soup with Walnut
        Pesto, **30**, 31
    Carrot and Ginger Soup, 32
    Cauliflower-Leek Soup with Madras
        Curry and Almonds, 27
    Yellow Split Pea Soup, 26
Soy sauce
    Clams Steamed in Sake with Soy
        and Pine Nuts, **66**, 67
    Tuna Cubes with Citrus Soy, Chives,
        and Cucumber, 82, **83**
Spanish mackerel
    Grilled Spanish Mackerel with Black
        Olives, Tomatoes, and Pistou, 81
    Mackerel, Oranges, Mint, Chiles, and
        Lemon Agrumato, **84**, 85

Specific Carbohydrate Diet, xxii
Spice blends, xxx
Spices
    for accenting foods, xxviii
    hot, xxviii
    Pan-Roasted Mushrooms, Herbs,
        and Spices, 135
    Spice-Dusted Potatoes, 144
    for sweetening foods, xxvii
Spigarello
    Grilled Sea Bass with Spigarello,
        Chiles, and Garlic, 89
Spinach
    Grilled Sea Bream with Lemon
        Gremolata and Spinach, 90, **91**
Squash
    Acorn Squash, Hazelnuts, Parmesan,
        and Acacia Honey, 146, **147**
    Acorn Squash Soup with Pistachios,
        Black Bread, and Apples, 28,
        29
    Autumn on a Plate, 12, **13**
    Butternut Squash Soup with Walnut
        Pesto, **30**, 31
    Five Fat Challenge: Salmon Avocado
        Caponata with Pistachios and
        Black Olive Oil, **78**, 79
Squid
    Seafood Boudin, 70–71
    Shrimp Semi-Ceviche Cara Cara, 65
    Squid Confit with White Bean
        Stifado, 69
Stew
    Squid Confit with White Bean
        Stifado, 69
Stifado
    Squid Confit with White Bean
        Stifado, 69
Strawberries
    Strawberries, Fennel, and Cucumber
        Salad, 10, 11
String beans
    Charred String Beans with Tofu-
        Miso Dressing, **136**, 137
    Tons of Crunch Summer Bean Salad,
        7
Striped bass
    Grilled Striped Bass with Sweet
        Peppers, New Potatoes, and
        Pesto, **92**, 93
Sugar snap peas
    Roasted Sugar Snaps, 172
Sumac
    Roasted Carrots with Sumac,
        Lemon, and Honey, **148**, 149

Sweeteners, xxxiii
Sweet potatoes
    Baked Sweet Potatoes, Granny
        Smith Apples, Chives, and
        Walnuts, 140
    Caramelized Sweet Potatoes with
        Smoked Sea Salt and
        Pecorino, 138, **139**
    Crisp-Baked Sweet Potatoes, 141

T

Tabbouleh
    Quinoa Tabbouleh with Feta Cheese
        and Cucumber, **38**, 39
"Tall Food" era, xvii
Thyme
    Slow-Roasted Organic Chicken with
        Parsley, Sage, Rosemary, and
        Thyme, 98, **99**
Tofu
    Charred String Beans with Tofu-
        Miso Dressing, **136**, 137
Tomatoes
    Beef Tartare with Capers, Pistachio
        Pesto, and Watermelon-
        Tomato Salad, 107–8, **109**
    Blistered Fairytale Eggplant Stewed
        in Olive Oil, Cherry Tomatoes,
        and Herbs, 123
    Five Fat Challenge: Salmon Avocado
        Caponata with Pistachios and
        Black Olive Oil, **78**, 79
    Grilled Chicken with Tomato Jam,
        100
    Grilled Spanish Mackerel with Black
        Olives, Tomatoes, and Pistou,
        81
    Grilled Turkey, Avocado, and
        Tomato on Seven Grain, 106
    Heirloom Tomatoes, Avocado,
        Mango, and Cucumber, 8, **9**
    Olive Oil–Poached Cod with
        Roasted Tomato and Peppers,
        86, **87**, 88
    Puffed Millet, Tomatoes, Jalapeño,
        and Avocado, 46, 47
Trans fat, xvi
Tuna
    Tokyo/Vietnam Tuna Wrap, 80
    Tuna Cubes with Citrus Soy, Chives,
        and Cucumber, 82, **83**
Turkey
    Grilled Turkey, Avocado, and
        Tomato on Seven Grain, 106

U

Unsaturated fat, sources of, xvi, xix
Unsaturated fats, sources of. *See also* Monounsaturated fats, sources of

V

Vegetables. *See also specific vegetables*
  cooked, 117–19
    Acorn Squash, Hazelnuts, Parmesan, and Acacia Honey, 146, **147**
    Baked Sweet Potatoes, Granny Smith Apples, Chives, and Walnuts, 140
    Blistered Broccoli with Garlic and Chiles, 131, **132–33**
    Blistered Fairytale Eggplant Stewed in Olive Oil, Cherry Tomatoes, and Herbs, 123
    Caramelized Sweet Potatoes with Smoked Sea Salt and Pecorino, 138, **139**
    Cauliflower Couscous with Fresh Herbs, Currants, and Coconut, 120
    Charred Eggplant, Grilled Onions, Pickled Raisins, and Pine Nuts, 122
    Charred String Beans with Tofu-Miso Dressing, **136**, 137
    Crisp-Baked Sweet Potatoes, 141
    Curried Beets, Apple, Fried Shallots, and Walnuts, 121
    Grilled Portobello Mushroom Sandwiches with Arugula and Date-Walnut Pesto, 134
    Pan-Roasted Brussels Sprouts with Southeast Asian Flavors, 128, **129**
    Pan-Roasted Mushrooms, Herbs, and Spices, 135
    Peppers Stewed in Olive Oil, Herbs, and Garlic, 124
    Portuguese Potatoes, **142**, 143
    Pumpkin Fries, 145
    Roasted Carrots with Cumin and Avocado, 150
    Roasted Carrots with Sumac, Lemon, and Honey, **148**, 149
    Sautéed Broccoli with Garlic and Chiles, 130
    Slow-Cooked Fennel in Olive Oil, 125, **126–27**
    Spice-Dusted Potatoes, 144
  craving for, x
  in salads, 1
Vinaigrette
  Grilled Salmon, Lentils, Avocado, and Pecans, with Sherry Vinaigrette, 77
Vinegars, for enhancing flavor, xxx
Vinho verde
  Stewed Clams and Mussels with Garlic and Vinho Verde, 68

W

Walnuts
  Baked Apples with Walnuts and Raisins, 156
  Baked Sweet Potatoes, Granny Smith Apples, Chives, and Walnuts, 140
  Butternut Squash Soup with Walnut Pesto, **30**, 31
  Curried Beets, Apple, Fried Shallots, and Walnuts, 121
  Date and Walnut Cookies, 158
  food combinations with, xxxii
  Grilled Portobello Mushroom Sandwiches with Arugula and Date-Walnut Pesto, 134
  Sweet and Spiced Nuts, 170, **171**
Walzog, David, xvii
Watermelon
  Beef Tartare with Capers, Pistachio Pesto, and Watermelon-Tomato Salad, 107–8, **109**
Waxman, Jonathan, ix–xii
Weight control, nuts for, xxii
Weight loss, dietary changes for, xviii
Wild rice, x
  Wild Rice Salad with Kale, Pecans, and Oranges, 50
Wraps
  Barbecue Chicken Wraps with Celery and Bean Sprouts, 104
  Tokyo/Vietnam Tuna Wrap, 80

Y

Yellow split peas
  Yellow Split Pea Soup, 26
Yellow wax beans
  Tons of Crunch Summer Bean Salad, 7

Z

Zatarain's Crawfish, Shrimp, & Crab Boil, xxx

Notes

Notes

Notes

Notes

Notes